The Life and Times of
Deshbandhu Chittaranjan Das

The Life and times of
Deshbandhu Chittaranjan Das

Nandini Saraf

Ocean Books Pvt. Ltd.
ISO 9001:2015 Publishers

Published by
Ocean Books (P) Ltd.
4/19 Asaf Ali Road,
New Delhi-110 002 (INDIA)
e-mail: info@oceanbooks.in

ISBN 978-81-8430-213-4
The Life and Times of
DESHBANDHU CHITTARANJAN DAS
by Nandini Saraf

Edition
2025

Price
₹ 350.00 (Rupees Three Hundred Fifty only)

Printed at
Shree Sai Printers, Sahibabad

Dedicated to

MRS. ADITI MUKERJEA (AMMA)

(Granddaughter of Chittaranjan Das)

Contents

PREFACE

The author interviewed Mrs. Aditi Mukerjea, the granddaughter of Deshbandhu Chittaranjan Das. She is residing in Kolkata, in an apartment named, 'Indrani' built on one of the plots of Mr. Dasand owned by her. The building was named Indrani, after the youngest sister of Mrs. Mukerjea's. She had another sister, Ms. Swarupa Das, who died a few years ago. Mrs. Mukerjea is the eldest daughter of Sujata Devi and Chirarajan Das, the only son of Chittaranjan Das.

1

DESHBANDHU CHITTARANJAN DAS

"If I die in this work of winning freedom, I believe I shall be born in this country again and again, live for it, hope for it, work for it with all the energy of my life, with all the love of my nature till I see the fulfilment of my hope and the realization of this idea."

These words of Chittaranjan Das, who died at the age of 54, in June 1925, in his pursuit of freeing India from the clutches of the British Empire, still resonate through the streets of Bengal where he was a hero amongst the middle and the poor classes of the society.

Chittaranjan Das was fondly known as "Deshbandhu" which means 'Friend of the Nation'. This name was given to him in 1922, long after he had proved himself a successful lawyer who defended Aurobindo Ghose in the celebrated Alipore Bomb Case (May 1908-May 1909).

Apart from his profession of a lawyer. Chittaranjan Das was also a poet at heart. He published many books of his poems and essays. The most renowned is *Sagar Sangeet*, published in 1913. This was translated into English language by Aurobindo Ghose titled, *The Song of the Seas*.

Above all this, Chittaranjan Das was a patriot. He dedicated his entire life toward his biggest dream—to attain 'Swaraj' or Self-Governance for the country; although it is disheartening to know that he did not live long enough to experience it. He was successful to some extent in this work and in order to fulfil his dream, he established the Swaraj Party in December 1922, along with Narasimha Chintaman Kelkar and Motilal Nehru.

Chittaranjan Das spent his life helping the poor and needy and his down-to-earth nature, which he inherited from his father, Bhubhamohan Das, compelled him to donate almost all his land for the establishment of hospitals and educational institutions for the poor.

Today, when one speaks of Chittaranjan Das, it is his pseudonym, 'Deshbandhu' which is used, because he was in the truest sense a friend of the nation.

❑

2

CHITTARANJAN: THE FREEDOM FIGHTER

"The difficulty is the European Association.... In the days of the Ilbert Bill Agitation, we saw what the Anglo-Indians could do. But then, public opinion was hardly born in this country. Today, again, when the British Government recognised the policy of Self-Government we hear the same uproar. These people who come here to make money, who come here penniless and when they retire, take away thousands and thousands—these people pretend to talk in the name of India when they say that these gentlemen should not be released because they know if they are released, they will strengthen the party which seeks Self-Government, because they know that when Mr. Mahomad Ali comes out, when Babu Sham Sunder Chakravarty comes out, they will fight shoulder to shoulder for the cause of Self-Government in this country. And if Self-Government is granted what about the policy of these merchants? If Self-Government is granted the authority of Magistrates and Collectors in every district will be lessened and then what would happen to these gentlemen who write letters to Collectors saying—my dear so and so, will you see this done and will you see that done? It is a notorious fact that in this country and I have heard complaints from many Indian Merchants engaged in coal trade that they cannot get wagons at a time when English merchants are fully supplied with wagons. These are the advantages which they get by this country being ruled not by the people of this country but by a bureaucracy. That really is the reason of this Anglo-Indian agitation.

"I must refer to the speeches made by these knights of Anglo-India against the interests of this country and against the policy of Self-Government. I will first of all refer to the foolish speech of Arden Wood. This gentleman is reported to have said: 'If racial feeling is to be dominant in Indian politics the time will come when we, the British, will either have to leave India or re-conquer it.' Now, gentleman, it is difficult to take this speech seriously.... They may stay in India if they find it profitable to do so but the tall of reconquering India is a comical statement...he ought to know that India was never conquered. India was won by love and won by promise of good government. India was never conquered and God willing, it will never be conquered for all time to come. India will impress her ideal, her civilization, and her culture upon the whole world. The work has commenced today. It will go on increasing till the world will listen to the message of India.

"Some of the other speakers made very angry speeches. One gentleman is reported to have said that if there is a government by the people and for the people then there will be no security for life and 'prosperity'. Mark the word prosperity. I do not know whether the printer's devil is responsible for this but if he is, this devil has got perfect knowledge of the internal affairs. The apprehension of this speaker is that if there is Self-Government, there will be no security or prosperity. Whose prosperity may we ask? Is it the prosperity of India, is it the prosperity of the teeming millions of our country or is it the prosperity of Sir Archie Birkmyre? Whose prosperity? If the granting of Home Rule to this country means the poverty of Sir Archie Birkmyre, let it be so, but still Self-Government must be granted. India does not live for Sir Archie Birkmyre or the petty traders who come here and rob us of our money. India lives for herself—she has lived for herself for centuries and she will live in herself and for herself for all the time to come. There is another statement made by this angry speaker, which takes my breath away. He says that this agitation of the European Association is to assert the rights of the British in India. The rights of the British in India! These little-minded traders who at a time when the Government enjoins a calm atmosphere hold a meeting and proceed straightaway to denounce the whole country; and abuse the people and all the ideals for which they fight and in which they live and move and have their being—these men claim the right to represent the British. The British indeed! When His Majesty's ministers say that there should be Home Rule, there should be Self-Government that the people of this country should be granted equal partnership with the people of England in the Empire, who are these traders who claim to represent British interests in India? Gentlemen, I will not take you through the many comical statements made by this entertaining band of players, Jones-Birkmyre Company. They are used to many tricks. I will refer to some of the *Statesman* newspaper, which used to pose as the Friend of India at one time. I think it has given up all that pretence now. This *Statesman* came out one day with a furious article on the Extremists of Bengal and praised the Moderates and the next day it said that there did not seem to be any difference between the Extremists and the Moderates. Well, the reason for that is quite clear. There is, in fact, no difference. This distinction was invented by the *Statesman* newspaper some years ago. We can frankly tell the Anglo-Indian community that there are no Extremists among us, no Moderates. The Hindus and Mahomedans of Bengal are all Nationalists—they are neither Extremists nor Moderates. I may tell you who the Extremists are. It is those Anglo-Indian Agitators who are the worst Extremists. You talk of a calm atmosphere! Who broke that calm? It is you Anglo-Indian agitators. It is Sir Hugh Bray, it is the Lieutenant Governor of the Punjab, it is the speakers who spoke at the meeting of the European Association. These people broke the calm. I ask them to consider the position and beware. Their days of the Ilbert Bill have gone by. These are the days of rising Democracy in this country. We will no longer tolerate that sort of vapourings, that kind of abuse. If, in spite of that, they persist in their wicked agitation, we shall soon know—how to deal with them. We are fighting in the best interests of the Empire; we are fighting for carrying out that very policy which has been declared in England by His Majesty's ministers, and by His Excellency the Viceroy in this country. If you dare stand against that, we will know how to deal with you. Be assured, we Indians do not deny your legitimate share whatever may be the extent of that share in the Government of this country. We know what you mean when you say that Self-Government is no good, because Self-Government would be against the interests of the teeming millions of India. We know the hollowness of that hypocrisy. But we can tell these gentlemen, so far as I am concerned, at any rate, I am perfectly clear, that we shall accept no Self-Government, no Home Rule unless it recognises and includes within it the teeming millions of India. When I ask for Home Rule, for Self-Government, I am not asking for another bureaucracy, another oligarchy in the place of the bureaucracy that there is at present. In my opinion, bureaucracy is bureaucracy, be that bureaucracy of Englishmen or of Anglo-Indians or of Indians. We want no bureaucracy, we want Home Rule, we want Self-Government by the people and for the people. We want Self-Government in which every individual of this country, be he the poorest ryot or the richest zamindar—will have his legitimate share. Every individual must have some voice. We want Home Rule broadly based on the will of the people of India. Now gentlemen, this is our objective. Do they still say or can they, in reason, say that we are not asking Home Rule on behalf and in the interests of the teeming millions of India? If they say we have got no right to ask for it in their interest, my answer is we have a thousand times greater right to ask for them than you who never know them or care for them. India has always been tolerant towards those people, whatever their religious creed or faith may be, who have made India their Home—every one of them is my brother and I embrace him with open arms. The history of India has made it abundantly clear. We have the Parsis in India. They adopted India as their home and today we embrace them as our brothers. We have had hosts of Mahomedan invaders who came to this country as conquerors but they made this country their home and today we embrace them with open arms. If these Anglo-Indians want to make India their home, let them do so and we will work hand in hand with them in the interest of the Indian Empire. But if they come here to make money and all their interests, it is how best to make it. I say they are no friends of India, they have got no right to call themselves Indians, they have got no legitimate right to oppose the granting of self-good to the people of India. I say to them. 'Come here if you want. Make money if you can. Go away in peace if you want to do so.'

"I said that our difficulty is the mischievous working of the European association. Let us be united, gentlemen. Let us assist the Government against this selfish and unreal agitation. I feel sure the victory is ours" (Grover, 1994).

This was the Presidential address which Chittaranjan Das gave at the Hindu-Mahomedan Mass Meeting held in Calcutta in October 1917. This meeting was held to protest against the internment of the brothers, Mohamad Ali and Shaukat Ali, who were imprisoned for four years for their pro-Turkish activities.

Chittaranjan Das, whom one knows as the great freedom fighter of India, was a simple man. He was a lawyer by profession, and an extreme romantic, who loved his nation and its people as much as he loved his family. His poetries are a proof of how emotional he was as a person, who felt deeply for everyone he was attached to.

"I have loved this land of mine with all my heart, from childhood; in manhood, through all my manifold weakness, unfitness and poverty of soul. I have striven to keep alive its image in my heart; and to-day, on the threshold of age, that image has become truer and clearer than ever."

These words, spoken by Chittaranjan, are evidence of his love for his nation.

Little known is the fact that Chittaranjan religiously followed the Hindu tradition. Everyone who has read his poems knows that he followed Vaishnava philosophy during his later life. But the fact that he belonged to a family of Brahmo believers and was still not accepted by the Samaj, reveals a great deal about him. Brahmo believers were supposed to be modern in their views and when Chittaranjan showed traits of 'orthodox' beliefs, they completely rejected him as a part of their Samaj.

❑

3

Birth and Education

The Das family belongs to the Vaidya caste (upper middle class) and their ancestral home was situated in Telirbag village, in Vikrampur, in the eastern part of Bengal. This is now a part of Bangladesh.

Kashiswar Das, grandfather of Chittaranjan Das, was quite a respectable and prominent man in the village. He had three sons, Durgamohan, Kalimohan and Bhubhamohan. They were all followers of Brahmo Samaj, after they renounced Hindu religion.

Bhubhamohan was married to Nistarini Devi and they lived in Calcutta, where Bhubhamohan was a solicitor at the Calcutta High Court. Chittaranjan was born here on November 5, 1870 in a rented house at Pataldanga Street. Soon Bhubhamohan shifted to Peepalpatty Road in Bhawanipur into his own house.

Here, Chittaranjan was admitted to London Missionary School in Standard VI after being assessed by Father Johnson, although he had applied for Standard VII (Sen, 1989). London Missionary School was supposed to be an institution for the poorer sections of the society and it was not a place where Bhubhamohan's son should have studied. But he had a different opinion about it. He wanted his son to know how the poor people lived and managed their lives. He wanted his son to be grounded and not be proud to belong to a rich family.

This helped Chittaranjan later, because he supported the cause of the poor, especially after he became a national figure.

In the meantime, Bhubhamohan's brother, Durgamohan Das, a lawyer in Barisal, came to Calcutta to establish himself after the Calcutta High Court was set up in 1861. When his wife died, he came to live in his brother's house. He had three sons, Satyaranjan, Jyotishranjan and Satishranjan and three daughters, Sarala, Abala and Sailabala. Satyaranjan grew up to become a Judge at Rangoon Court. Satishranjan became a law member of the Vice-Regal Council and the founder of Doon School. Sarala Roy founded the Gokhale Memorial School and Lady Abala Bose married the famous scientist, Jagdish Chandra Bose.

Mrs. Mukerjea, the granddaughter of Chittaranjan, narrated their family's history in these words,

"Everyone lived in the same house; my grandfather's cousins and his own siblings. He had two brothers and five sisters, among whom, he was the eldest. One of his brothers, Basantaranjan, was adopted by Kalimohan Das, who had no sons. Prafullaranjan was the other brother of Chittaranjan, who later became an established lawyer, and was famous all over India. His eldest sister, Tarala Gupta was widowed early with six children and came to live in their house after his uncle moved out. Amala Das never married. She was a friend of Tagore and she prepared tunes for his songs; this was mentioned in

Tagore's son, Rathindranath's book. Urmila Devi went to jail with my grandmother. She was a freedom fighter. The other two sisters were suitably married."

Bhubhamohan was a very generous man, who felt for the poor and needy and he did whatever he could to help them from time to time. This led him to insolvency and was declared insolvent by the court. This same trait was seen even in Chittaranjan.

As it has already been established, Chittaranjan did not specialise in just one thing. He was an all-rounder. His interest in reading and writing poetry, amongst other things, displayed his sensitive nature. His favourite poets during his early days were Rangalal Banerjee and Hemchandra Banerjee; their poems had a patriotic fervour in them. Chittaranjan's own poems reflected what he thought about his country.

He was both an idealist and a realist, a combination rarely seen, yet it is a blend that marked him as a cautious and ambitious boy.

After finishing school, Chittaranjan passed the Entrance Examination of Presidency College. He was popular in school therefore, as soon as he entered college; he became a prominent member of the Student's Association, which was headed by Surendranath Banerjee.

However, Chittaranjan had to quit the Association after graduation in 1890 from Presidency College. He was not given his Honours degree because he had missed one year. He had to appear for his exams in 1889, but could not owing to some unavoidable circumstances.

Then, he went to England to train for the Indian Civil Service Examinations. In 1892, he appeared for the exams but failed. During his stay in England, he met Dadabhai Naoroji, who was competing for a seat in the British House of Commons for Central Finsbury.

Chittaranjan already a patriot at heart had not to be urged. He started campaigning for Dadabhai without requests from the former and organised meetings where he delivered a few lectures. This attracted a large audience which was impressed by his speech. This was when he was in his early twenties!

During this time, James Maclean made some hateful remarks regarding India; he stated that since it was conquered by sword, it can only be retained by sword. Chittaranjan was furious and in reply gave a speech at the meeting in Oldham, headed by W.E. Gladstone, in which he said,

"Gentlemen, I was sorry to find it given expression to in Parliamentary speeches on more than one occasion that England conquered India by the sword, and by the sword must she keep it. England, Gentlemen, did no such thing, it was not her swords and bayonets that won for her this vast and glorious Empire; it was not her military valour that achieved this triumph, it was in the main a moral victory or a moral triumph. England might well be proud of it. But to attribute all this to the sword and then to argue that the policy of sword is the only policy that ought to be pursued in India is to my mind absolutely base and quite unworthy of an Englishman" (Ray, 1927).

A leader was born and everyone could see the elements of a great man in the making. His speeches were published in the papers and his oratory skills were appreciated by everyone, both in India and abroad.

After failing in the Indian Civil Service Examination, Chittaranjan joined Middle Temple and within a few months, he was called to the English Bar. He had been studying law during this time with more dedication than he had put into the Civil Service exams.

Chittaranjan came back to India in 1893 and registered himself as a Barrister at the Calcutta High Court. He did not find success immediately. There were many eminent personalities at the Bar at that time, and since his father had already retired, he too could not help him out (Ray, 1927).

This gave Chittaranjan enough time to start writing poems and letters. Shortly, *Malancha*, his first book of poems was published in 1895. It received a great deal of criticism from members of the Brahmo Samaj. *Malancha* is a collection of fifty-three poems. Mainly, the complaints which were put forward were that the poems in this collection were immoral and did not touch emotionally.

❑

4

A Poet and a Romantic

In 1897, on December 3, Chittaranjan married Basanti Devi. She was the daughter of Barada Nath Halder, who was the Dewan of Bijni estate in Assam. He was also a social reformer who joined the Brahmo Samaj. He would rescue young girls too young to be married, and put them in schools, their rightful place.

It is an interesting how they first met. This was narrated to the author by Chittaranjan's granddaughter.

Chittaranjan was around twenty-seven and she was only seventeen when they got married. When their parents fixed their marriage, both refused and did not even want to see each other. Basanti Devi wanted to study further so her father asked her to at least see the man. Chittaranjan's parents also wanted him to meet Basanti Devi once. So one day, his parents took him to her uncle's house but he tried to avoid the meeting by taking the backstairs. At the same time, when Basanti Devi got to know that he was coming to meet her, she too, took the backstairs to avoid meeting him. As luck would have it, they saw each other for the first time on the stairs. This incident led them gradually to accept each other. Their marriage seemed inevitable.

The ceremony took place according to the Brahmo rituals, but no one from the Brahmo Samaj was present at the wedding; Mrs. Mukerjea remembers her grandmother telling her that on her wedding day, she was wearing a *ghunghat*, so she tried to see who all had come to bless them, and could not find even a single Brahmo member.

Chittaranjan's poems had perhaps distanced them from him, but as far as he was concerned, he was unperturbed by their rejection.

Chittaranjan and Basanti Devi had their first child, Aparna in 1898; then in 1899, their son Chiraranjan and two years later in 1901, their second daughter, Kalyani.

Chittaranjan was a romantic, and his love was not merely reserved for his country and family.

All this while, he was busy writing and practicing law. While in the former, he achieved some name, the latter still needed more of his time and energy. He published his second book of songs, *Mala*, in 1904. This received a great deal of appreciation from Aurobindo Ghose and these poems were even compared to Rabindranath Tagore's *Gitanjali*.

A few lines from one of the songs from *Mala* are given here,

> In the surrounding twilight, thou hast put
> A lighted taper on thy window-sill:
> All my mind takes light
> From the golden light of thy taper! (Ray, 1927)

Chittaranjan and his family also had to face a great deal of financial problem during this time. His father was not well and they were under enormous debts. They entered the Insolvency Court in June 1906 in the hope of obtaining relief.

Meanwhile, Chittaranjan joined *Bande Matram*, an English weekly, which had Aurobindo Ghose as its *de facto* editor. This paper mainly appealed to the patriotic masses of the country and was a rage in Bengal.

During this time, Basantaranjan, one of his brothers, who had been adopted by his uncle, Kalimohan, suddenly died. He left behind all his property to their mother, Nistarini Devi. In her Will, she divided her wealth and land equally between her two sons, Prafullaranjan and Chittaranjan.

Prafullaranjan, in turn, later sold his property to his brother. Hence, within a few years Chittaranjan inherited a large area of land and great wealth.

Between May 1908 and May 1909, Chittaranjan was busy with the Alipore Bomb Conspiracy Case defending his friend, Aurobindo Ghose. Mr. Ghose was ultimately acquitted and after this case Chittaranjan became a high profile lawyer.

He published *Sagar Sangeet* (Bengali) in 1913, which is his most celebrated book of poems till date. It was translated into English by Mr. Ghose, who needed some money urgently and Chittaranjan helped him by letting him translate his book for a sum of thousand rupees. Some verses from the translated book, *The Songs of the Sea*, are as follows.

The Songs of the Sea

I

O thou unhoped-for elusive wonder of the skies,
Stand still one moment! I will lead thee and bind
With music to the chambers of my mind.
Behold how calm today this sea before me lies
And quivering with what tremulous heart of dreams
In the pale glimmer of the faint moonbeams.
If thou at last art come indeed, O mystery, stay

Woven by song into my heart-beats from this day.
Stand, goddess, yet! Into this anthem of the seas
With the pure strain of my full voiceless heart
Some rhythm of the rhythmless, some part
Of thee I would weave today, with living harmonies
Peopling the solitude I am within.
Wilt thou not here abide on that vast scene,
Thou whose vague raiment edged with dream
haunts us and flees,
Fulfilled in an eternal quiet like this sea's?

II

I lean to thee a listening ear
And thy immense refrain I hear,
O Ocean circled with the lights of morn.
What word is it thou singst? What tune
My heart is filled with, and it soon
Must overflow? What mystical unborn
Spirit is singing in thy white foam-caves?
What voice turns heaven to music from thy waves?

XL

This shore and that shore,—I am tired, they pall.
Where thou art shoreless, take me from it all.
My spirit goes floating and can find oppressed
In thy unbanked immensity only rest.
Thick darkness falls upon my outer part,
A lonely stillness grips the labouring heart,
Dumb weeping with no tears to ease the eyes.
I am mad for thee, O king of mysteries.
Have I not sought thee on a million streams,
And wheresoever the voice of music dreams,
In wondrous lights and sealing shadows caught,
And every night and every day have sought?
Pilot eternal, friend unknown embraced,

O, take me to thy shoreless self at last. (Ghose)

The poet in Chittaranjan appeals to the sound that the sea makes, which brings him so much peace that he wishes to be bound by it forever. But, in the last song, the poet said that he is tired of the deaths and rebirths and prays to God to free him from such a life and let him return to Him.

Chittaranjan was a family man. He believed in the Joint Family system, unlike the members of the Brahmo Samaj of that time. In the words of his granddaughter:

"We lived in a joint family. My grandfather's mother, brother and wife, and children; all of us lived in the same house. My grandfather's eldest sister was widowed with five children, and so, even they came to live with us. The food used to be cooked in a huge *handi*, because there were so many people. There were always poor students eating in our house."

He wrote more poems in the next few years. His *Antaryami* was published in 1915 and *Kishore-Kishore* in 1916. These reflected his Vaishnava beliefs, which he had started following religiously. No wonder, the members of Brahmo Samaj criticised him for these poems.

Chittaranjan also started a monthly journal *Narayan*, and great writers, like Sarat Chandra Chatterjee, Bipin Chandra Pal and Hariprasad Shastri, contributed to this paper. Sometimes, the articles and poems by some writer or the other were criticised. Chittaranjan was unaffected by such criticisms and told everyone to remove dirt from their minds, instead of finding dirt in these works (Sen, 1989).

Gradually, Chittaranjan was gaining popularity as both a lawyer and a poet. He was also flourishing as an orator, something which he had started when he was quite young. He was called to meetings to speak and people were impressed by his patriotism.

Chittaranjan was never a follower of the Brahmo Samaj. It was mainly because his parents influence. His father was a poet too, which explains Chittaranjan's inclination toward poetry; and his mother's dream was that her son frees India from the foreign rule, hence the loyalty toward his nation. His parents were attached to their extended family who were all quite orthodox in their thoughts and practices and therefore this inspired Chittaranjan greatly and explains why he turned his attention toward Vaishnava philosophy later in his life.

❑

5

CHITTARANJAN: THE LAWYER

Chittaranjan was not well known as a lawyer, when he was asked to defend Aurobindo Ghose in the Alipore Bomb Case. Prior to this, he had defended Brahmab Bandhab Upadhyay and Bipin Chandra Pal in 1907 and was also involved with the Khururia Zamindari Case, but without much success.

Brahmabandhab Upadhyay, who was involved in the case of sedition, had actually refused to be defended. Mr. Upadhyay had even given a written statement saying, "I do not want to take part in the trial, because I do not believe that, in carrying out my humble share of the God-appointed mission of Swaraj, I am in any way accountable to the alien people, who happen to rule over us and whose interest is, and must necessarily be, in the way of our true national development."

However, while his trial was going on, Mr. Upadhyay died suddenly in Campbell Hospital in Calcutta and the case was closed.

Chittaranjan also defended Bhupendra Nath Dutta, who too was charged with sedition. He was the editor of *Yugantar*. Although they lost the case and Mr. Dutta was imprisoned for one year, Chittaranjan was still praised for the way he handled the case.

Thereafter, he was given the case of Alipore Bomb Conspiracy Case.

On April 30, 1908, Khudiram Bose and Prafulla Chakki threw a bomb at a carriage in Muzzafarpur. They belonged to a revolutionary organisation in Manicktolla. The intention was to kill Mr. Kingsford, who was a District Judge; but instead it killed two women who were travelling in that carriage, they were the wife and daughter of Mr. Pringle Kennedy.

This sensationalised the case and the police started taking active part in finding out the bomber. Soon, they discovered a bomb factory in Manicktolla and arrested thirty-six men for the same, in which Aurobindo Ghose was one of them. They alleged the setting of the bomb factory to be a part of a conspiracy against the King.

Aurobindo Ghose had come to India after having studied at St. Pauls School in London and later in Cambridge. In India, he came as the Vice-Principal of Baroda College and was there till 1906. This was the time when the Partition of Bengal had recently tormented the people and had instigated a patriotic fire within them. *Bande Matram*, an English Weekly started its publication from August 6, 1906 in Calcutta and Mr. Ghose decided to join it. He worked as the editor in the weekly, contributing to it as much as he could (Ray, 1927).

Many a times, the articles of the weekly were too outrageous in terms of patriotism and were often criticised. Aurobindo was even arrested once on charge of sedition but at that time, he was acquitted because he was not the official editor of the paper. However, the police did keep a check on him, because they thought that his articles were influencing people to take dangerous measures against the Empire.

The trial for the bomb conspiracy case took place before the Magistrate of Alipore and began on May 19, 1908 (Ray, 1927). The defence lawyer who represented the thirty-six men was too expensive for them; hence they had to find another lawyer. Chittaranjan Das was recommended by Aurobindo Ghose and the former immediately stood up for him. He was happy to represent him in the case and since the accused did not have any money to give, Chittaranjan did not even ask for it. For one whole year, he took up no other case and concentrated totally on Mr. Ghose's trial.

Mr. Ghose was arrested because they found some letters and articles written by him to his wife and friends, which Mr. Norton, who was representing the Crown, tried to prove as evidence for the bomb conspiracy.

In defence, Chittaranjan presented this speech before the Magistrate,

"So far as the nation was concerned, he (Aurobindo) preached that lofty ideal of freedom. So far as the individual was concerned, his idea always was to go there himself and look for the Godhead within. It is a familiar ideal of our country. It is difficult for those not familiar with it to understand it.

The doctrine of Vedantism is that man is not dissociated from God: that is to say, if you want to realize yourself you must look for the God within you. It is within your heart and within your soul that you will find that God dwells, and as no man can attain to his own salvation without reaching to that God that is within you; so also in the case of nations: without any national question arising—no nation can attain this unless it realises the highest and noblest and the best of that nation. As in the case of individuals you cannot reach your God with extraneous aid, but you must make an effort—that supreme effort—yourself before you can realize the God within you; so also with a nation. It is by itself that a nation must grow; a nation must attain its salvation by its unaided effort. No foreigner can give you that salvation. It is within your own hands to revive that spirit of nationality. That is the doctrine of nationality which Aurobindo has preached throughout and that was to be done, not by methods which are against the traditions of the country. I ask your particular attention to that. It was not Aurobindo's philosophy that salvation was to be attained by methods inconsistent with the whole history and traditions of the writer, and therefore, when you find Aurobindo leaving Baroda and coming to Calcutta you find that the doctrines he preaches are not doctrines of violence but doctrines of passive resistance. It is not bombs, but suffering. He deprecates secret societies and violence and enjoins them to suffer. If there is a law which is unjust and offensive against the development of the nation, break that law by all means and take the consequences. He never asked you to apply force in a single utterance of his either in the Press or on the platform. If the government thought fit to bring in a law which hinders you from attaining that salvation, Aurobindo's advice is to break that law if necessary in the sense of not obeying it. You owe it to your conscience; you owe it to your God. If the law says you must go to jail, go to jail. That was the cardinal feature of the doctrine of passive resistance which Aurobindo preached. Is not the doctrine of passive resistance preached throughout the world on the same footing? Is it peculiar to this country—this movement which has met with such abusive language from Mr. Norton? Have not the people of England done it over and over again? I say that this is the same doctrine that Aurobindo was preaching almost up to the very day when those handcuffs were put on his hands. He was oppressed with a feeling of disappointment, because his country was losing everything, having lost their faith. Therefore, you find, whenever he preached freedom, he brought out that feature clearly. He says, believe in yourself; no one attains salvation who does not believe in himself. Similarly, he says, in the case of the nation. If the nation does not feel that it has got something within it to be free to attain that salvation then there is no hope for that nation. Accordingly we find Aurobindo preaching 'you are not cowards, you are not a set of incapable men, because you have got divinity. Have faith in you and in that faith go towards that goal and become a self-developed nation.'"

The most important evidence was a letter written to Mr. Ghose by his younger brother, Barindra Kumar Ghose, who was the head of the revolutionary organisation of which Khudiram Bose and Prafulla Chakki were a part. The letter says,

Dear Brother,

Now is the time, please try and make them meet for our conference. We must have sweets all over India ready-made for emergencies; I wait here for your answer.

Your affectionate,
Barindra Kumar Ghose.

Mr. Norton was trying to prove that the word 'sweets' was actually used in place of bombs, whereas Chittaranjan very cleverly proved that the letter was false. He concluded his speech with the following words,

"The evidence as is furnished by the confession in this court—a confession, upon which the prosecution relies—you will find that it is childish conspiracy—a toy revolution. It is impossible that Aurobindo could ever believe in his heart of hearts that, by bombing one or two Englishmen or some Englishmen at different places, they could ever have been able to subvert the British Government. If you credit him with intellectual powers and say that he was a brilliant mind, it is open to you at the same time to say that he was the leader of a childish conspiracy and a toy revolution.

Either drop the suggestion that it is because of the intellectual powers, because of the brilliant qualities with which he is credited, that you want the court to believe that he was the leader of this conspiracy; or the other theory that he was in fact the leader of the conspiracy and of this alleged revolutionary project.

If the government has taken into its head to believe that there is a vast conspiracy which is threatening the stability of the government, it is common knowledge that you do come across spies who give false evidence. I shall just read a passage from a book written by an eminent judge: 'The government under these circumstances have spies, who wriggle into the case, eavesdrop into families, abstract correspondence and false letters.' Therefore the evidence given before you is evidence that you can expect in a case like this.

My appeal to you, therefore, is that a man like this, who is being charged with the offence with which he has been charged, stands not only before the bar in this Court, but stands before the bar of the High Court of History. My appeal to you is this, that long after the controversy will be hushed in silence, long after this turmoil, the agitation will have ceased, long after he is dead and gone, he will be looked upon as the poet of patriotism; as the prophet of nationalism and the lover of humanity. Long after he is dead and gone, his words will be echoed and re-echoed not only in India, but across distant seas and lands. Therefore, I say, that the man in his position is not only standing before the bar of this Court, but before the bar of the High Court of History.

The time has come for you, Sir, to consider your judgement, and for you, gentlemen (addressing the Assessors) to consider your verdict. I appeal to you, Sir, in the name of all the traditions of the English Bench that forms the most glorious chapter of English history. I appeal to you in the name of all that is noble, of all the thousand principles of law which have emanated from the English Bench, and I appeal to you in the name of the distinguished judges who have administered the law in such a manner as to compel not only obedience, but the respect of all those in whose cases they have administered the law. I appeal to you in the name of the glorious chapter of English history, and let it not be said that an English judge forgets to vindicate justice. To you, gentlemen, I appeal in the name of the very ideal that Aurobindo preached, and in the name of all the traditions of our country; and let it not be said that two of his own countrymen (referring to the Assessors) were overcome by passion and prejudice and yielded to the clamour of the moment" (Ray, 1927).

Thus, the case which was on trial for about one whole year came to an end and Mr. Ghose was acquitted. Chittaranjan's speech was highly praised and at once his skills as a lawyer came to the notice of everyone.

Mr. B.C. Chatterjee, a counsel, praised in *Forward* (tabloid started by Chittaranjan) about his skills in these words,

"Some fundamental qualities underlay his advocacy. He possessed iron strength and never yielded an inch of ground either to judge or to adversary; and combined with it a driving power of argument before which even hostile judges faltered, and ultimately fell. There was not the least trace of sycophancy in his pleading, nor the faintest of tremors at the knees in the presence of authority. He stood and spoke like a man to a fellow-man, but gave off all the time that unconscious magnetism which generally over-powered judge and audience. The most noteworthy feature of his advocacy was that its quality impressed in proportion to the difficulty of its subject matter."

Later Mr. Ghose too praised Chittaranjan in a speech which he gave at Uttarpada. Following is an extract from the speech.

"You have all heard the name of the man who put away his all other thoughts and abandoned all his practices, who sat up half the night day after day for months and broke his health to save me—Srijut Chittaranjan Das. When I saw him, I was satisfied; but I still thought it necessary to write instructions. Then all that was put from me and I had the message from within. This is the man who will save you from the snares put around your feet. Put aside those papers. It is not you who will instruct him. I will instruct him. From that time I did not myself speak a word to my counsel about the case or give a single instruction, and if ever I was asked a question. I always found that my answer did not help the case. I had left it to him and he took it entirely into his hands with what results you know" (*Deshbandhur Katha*, 1982, August 15).

Chittaranjan became a renowned lawyer in the country and suddenly everyone wanted him to help them with their cases. He paid off all his debts by 1913 and started earning more than he needed. Even with this busy schedule, Chittaranjan managed to write more poems and published two song books between 1914 and 1916.

❑

6

CHITTARANJAN: THE ALTRUIST

The more success Chittaranjan got, the more humble he became. He started giving away most of his earnings to charity which was not unusual, coming from the son of Bhubhamohan Das. It is said that whenever Chittaranjan used to come from office, there were people lined up in front of his house to ask him for help. He used to give away whatever he had in his pockets and more.

Chittaranjan started leading a lavish lifestyle. During the end of his life, he had a huge bungalow, with two kitchens and a big garden. There was also a small pond and a temple within the compound. A part of this plot of land now holds the Chittaranjan Seva Sadan. He had become one of the highest paid lawyers of India, with fifty thousand rupees per month as his salary.

When they had no money, after his father was declared insolvent during the first decade of 1900, Chittaranjan used to walk to and from the High Court since they had no transportation. This is the same man, who later, when he had the means, gave afternoon meal to poor children once they were back from school.

Such was his selflessness that one cannot even dream to achieve.

Mrs. Mukherjea recalls,

"The day Aurobindo's judgement came out and he was free, they all came to our house. That house is demolished now. But the temple is still there. There was also a big pond on our compound. So Aurobindo and others, who came to our house, all took a dip in the pond and prayed in that temple. My grandmother cooked rice for them in two large *handis* because they were in jail and they hadn't eaten proper food for days. My grandmother cooked all the things they liked. They were all so very young...."

"Grandmother told me, there was a Coolie Strike in Assam's tea garden area and Assam-Bengal railway employees were on hunger strike (1921). She and her husband along with some Congress workers were going to help them. On the way they had to cross a river by boat, but there was a problem because of the storm and heavy rain. The boatmen refused to go any further. But my grandfather was determined and said that we have to go there because they are on a hunger strike and they are not eating anything. So the boatmen told him to go straight on the road, where there was a railway station and they could board a train from there. So, my grandfather, grandmother and two other people started walking through the paddy fields and then through a field which was just like a forest. After they crossed the field, they saw a flickering light in the distance and they walked toward it. There was a snake charmers catching snakes and they were sitting on a raised platform. Some people also lived nearby. My grandparents and others were all hungry and wet because of rain and these people offered them shelter. They even gave them clothes to wear and food to eat in the middle of the night. In those days, one had to light the coal *chulha* to cook food. They made some rice and *dal.* Grandmother said that was the best *dal* she ever ate in her life."

This little incident in Chittaranjan's life narrated by his wife to her grandchildren shows how concerned he was for the people of his country, that it seemed fit for him to take his wife and others through a jungle while it was raining heavily, in order to reach a place where he could help people who were on a hunger strike.

It also shows how Basanti Devi was a dedicated wife who supported him in everything that he did. Without her support, probably Chittaranjan Das could have achieved what he did, but would not have anyone to share it with.

❑

7

A Leader was Born

On April 21, 1917, right before the Declaration by Montague, the Secretary of State for Indian Affairs, on August 20, a Bengal Provincial Conference was held in Calcutta where Chittaranjan was asked to preside. He made his speech in Bengali, but it was also translated into English for the government.

Surendranath Banerjee had to invite Chittaranjan on stage for his monumental speech, but before he so invited him, he spoke highly of the President. He said,

"Mr. C.R. Das needs no introduction at my hands. At Bhowanipore he certainly needs none. In the rest of Bengal he hardly needs any. He is one of the most prominent leaders of the Bar, and if I am permitted to indulge in a bit of prophecy which is my birth-right by virtue of my Brahmanical position, I will say this that he will within a measurable distance of time become one of the most prominent leaders of public opinion in this Province."

Perhaps this prophecy of his came true, sooner than expected. The speech that Chittaranjan gave on that day is remembered even today as one of his most influential addresses of all times. An extract of it is:

"Today in this great assembly of Bengalis I have come to speak of Bengal.... I shall lay before you some of those things which have been simmering in my mind for a long time—things which I have realized more and more fully, through all the endeavours and experiences of life—things which I definitely and decisively accepted as 'true'...whether it is welcome or not.

"Some people might say: 'This Conference is for political discussion, what has talk about Bengal to do with it?' Such a question is symptomatic of our disease. To look upon life not as a comprehensive whole, but as divided among many compartments, was no part of our national culture and civilisation. We have borrowed this method from Europe and we have not understood what we have borrowed; and hence the failure of so much of our efforts and endeavour. The thing that we are accustomed to describe as Politics—has it no organic or intimate connection with the whole of Bengal or the whole of the Bengali people?... Must we divide life bit by bit like this?... Rather, must we not view our political discussions from the standpoint of the whole of our countrymen? And how shall we find truth unless we view life thus comprehensively and as a whole?

"What is politics? What is the object of this science?... the object of Political Science is to ascertain as to how much of political power should rest with the rulers and how much with the ruled, in order that the affairs of the country may be conducted in peace and harmony.

"But, after all, what is the ultimate object and significance, of this political thought and endeavour?... the object of our politics will be to build up the Bengalis into a nation of men. I would not admit for one moment that the Bengalis are wanting in manhood—nay, rather

I feel an inexpressible pride in describing myself as a Bengali. I know that the Bengali has a culture and philosophy of his own, that he has a Law, History, Philosophy and Literature of his own.

"... But we may take it for granted that the Bengalis have many faults which require to be corrected; and in that sense we may concede for argument that the Bengali is deficient in manhood. To correct this deficiency, to complete the manhood of Bengal must be the aim and endeavour of our political efforts, and it is therefore that we must discuss the precise relation between Sovereign and subject in this country. But in order to do this adequately, we shall have to ascertain precisely what our present condition is; and in order to ascertain this, we shall have to take first into consideration the material circumstances of our people. This again will require that we shall have to enquire into the condition of our peasantry—whether agricultural wealth is increasing or decreasing, and whether agriculture is flourishing or otherwise. This in its turn will lead us to a further enquiry still, as to why our people are leaving their villages in increasing numbers and are coming to settle within towns. Is it because the villages are insanitary, or is there any other reason for that?

"Thus we find that an adequate discussion of Politics will involve a consideration of agricultural question as well as the question of village sanitation.

"At the same time we shall have to consider whether we can improve our material condition even by bringing under village all the available cultivable land of the country. If we cannot, then we shall have to consider the question of industry and trade as well.

"To understand these questions, we shall have to consider what our agricultural and commercial methods were in the past and how we used to maintain the health of our villages.... We shall have to consider also the question of education and culture. How we trained ourselves in the past, how we used to diffuse education in the past and what the methods of present-day education must be; these should be discussed along with political questions.

"We shall have to consider further how our agriculture, our trade, our education were all connected in the past with our social system; and in the light of this knowledge, we must consider what their present relation to society must be.

".... We must consider also the precise relation in which all our thoughts, endeavours and activities stood and still stand with reference to the question of Religion; for I believe that we shall mis-read and mis-know all things, unless we keep this point steadily in view. If we disregard this aspect of things, all our problems will become unnecessarily hard and complex, and no solution will ever be possible for them.

"We have many dangers and difficulties in the path; but our chiefest danger is this that we have become largely and unnecessarily Anglicised in our education, culture and social practices. The mere mention of 'Polities' conjures up before our eyes the vision of English political institutions; and we feel tempted to fall down before and worship the precise form which Politics has assumed under the peculiar conditions of English History.... There is no end to our talk about schools and systems of politics, we learn by rote all the polished phrases that we can pick up from the texts and scriptures of European Politics; and fancying ourselves invincible in our panoply of learned phrases, we challenge the government to enter into a war of words with us.... We never look to our country; never think of Bengal or the Bengalis, of our past national history, or our present material condition. Hence, our political agitation is unreal and unsubstantial—divorced from all intimate touch with the soul of our people.

".... We boast of being educated; but how many are we? What room do we occupy in the country? What is our relation to the vast masses of our countrymen? Do they think our thoughts or speak our speech? I am bound to confess that our countrymen have little faith in us. And what is the reason of this unfaith? Down in the depths of our soul, we the educated people, have become Anglicised, we read in English, think in English and even our speech is translated from English. Our borrowed Anglicism repels our unsophisticated countrymen; they prefer the genuine article to the shoddy imitation. Besides we seem to look upon them with contempt. Do we invite them to our assemblies and our conferences? Perhaps we do, when we want their signatures to some petition to be submitted before the government, but do we associate with them heartily in any of our endeavour?... Let us then in all humility confess the truth and admit our gross and serious shortcomings in this matter. No trust, no right, can be based upon a falsehood; and hence I have said that our political agitation is a lifeless and soulless farce—a thing without reality and truth. No doubt we shall have to build it up into truth; but to do that we shall have to base it upon the life of Bengal; and hence it is that I propose in this great assembly to speak about my land, my home, this 'Banga-Bhumi' of ours.

".... Let us think for a moment of the fatal and universal weakness which had beset our people when the English first came to this land. Our Religion of Power—the Gospel of Sakti—had become a mockery of its former self; it had lost its soul of beneficence in the repetition of empty formulas and the observance of meaningless mummeries. Again, the Religion of Love with which *Mahaprabhu* had conquered the country—a religion which, like some mighty current of glory and light had swept with resistless force over the land and had borne strength and life whither soever it went—that religion too had become reduced to a barren clashing of beads. As with Religion, so it had happened with Knowledge; and the traditions of *Navadwip's* ancient glory and scholarship had become a mere name and memory. Thus, the Hindus of Bengal had lost strength and vigour, like in Religion, Science and Life. And the Musalmans also had similarly declined since the days of Alivardi; their strength and manhood had been swept away in that passion for luxury which is a sure mark of weakness and decadence.

"It was in this period of gloom and depression that the English tradesman came to India. He raised his empire in a world of ruins, and by rapid extension of power gave proof of his wonderful energy and vitality. To us it happened as it happens to all the weak. We accepted the English Government, and with that we accepted the English race—their culture, in their civilisation, their Luxury and their Licence...so we in the blindness of our misfortune, drifted away from the ancient landmarks of our soil—its History, its Culture, its Law and its Philosophy, and went in passionate pursuit of the Literature, Science and Philosophy of the English people. Perhaps this infatuation for things foreign has lessened in force; but we cannot claim that it has disappeared altogether.

"The trumpet of Science which Rammohan sounded at the threshold of national life—we heard it

—or we thought that we heard it; in any case we began repeating its cant formulas. But we cared little for that profound study of the *sastras* in which Rammohan had immersed himself; we overlooked altogether the fact that Rammohan had sought to find the path of our salvation in the midst of our national culture and civilisation. Time passed; schools and colleges came to be founded, and our bent towards Western civilisation became more marked still. Then, after long years, 'Bankim' came and set up the image of our Mother in the motherland.... He called unto the whole people and said: 'Behold, this is our Mother; worship her and establish her in your houses.' The song which he sang was of this Mother, 'well-watered, well-fruited, cool with the south breeze, green with the growing corn.' But we were deaf to the song that he sang, we were blind to the image that he saw, and hence Bankim lamented and said: 'I am crying alone in the wilderness.'

"Then came Sasadhar Tarkachuramani and the revival of Hinduism—a revival about the value of which there is considerable difference of opinion. There are some who say that it has been fruitful of much good, and there are others who think that it was wholly evil.

"..... The trumpet of 'Swadeshisin' began to sound in 1903. The people of Bengal began once more to understand and realise themselves. 'Rabindranath' sang: 'The soil of Bengal, the water of Bengal—make it true, oh Lord.' And as if in response to the poet's song, the soil and water of Bengal began to justify themselves.

"There are many wise, grave and reverent seniors among us who think—so I have heard—that the Swadeshi Agitation was a colossal blunder. Western education has given rise to a kind of soulless culture in our midst—a culture that is powerless for good but is ambitious of much. People who boast of this culture seek to measure all things by rule and scale, they are Pandits of Mathematics, and they reduce all questions to the level of mathematical problems. But the flood of life defies Mathematics; it sweeps away scale and balance. The Swadeshi Movement came like a tempest; it rushed along impetuously like some mighty flood.... And the great flood of life which we designate as the Swadeshi Movement—it submerged us, it swept us off our feet, but it revitalised our lives; it enabled us to come once more in contact with the living, vital soul of Bengal. Under its reviving influence we steeped ourselves once again in that stream of culture and civilisation which has been flowing perennially through the heart of Bengal; we were enabled once more to catch glimpses of the true continuity of our national history...we understood the significance of Rammohan's deep discipline; we recognised the image which Bankim worshipped and about which he sang: 'Thou art culture, and thou art law; thou art heart, and thou art soul; and thou art the breath of life in the body. In the arms thou art strength; in the heart thou art devotion and it is thy image, Mother, which we build in air our shrines;' Bankim's voice went through our ears and thrilled our hearts. We understood once again what it was that Ramakrishna sought and found.... We understood that the Bengali might be a Hindu or Musalman or Christian, but he continued to be a Bengali all the same; that he has a distinct type, a distinct character and a distinct law of his own. In this world of men, the Bengali has a place of his own—a claim, a culture and a duty.

"…. So, the main problem for our consideration is this—how to develop fully and adequately the newly awakened national life of Bengal; what measures may be necessary for it, and how to utilise them fully. But a difficulty has arisen at the very outset. Some Pandits in Europe are said to have discovered that the nation-idea is entirely imaginary; that there is no distinct basis for distinct nationalities; and ethnically no race is pure, but has received admixture from other races as well; that, further, owing to close and constant inter-communion between different races…. Stated thus, the thing reads like an old and venerable platitude: but it has got a new lease of life and has been proclaimed with some vigour since the outbreak of the present war. As a necessary consequence, some of our own people have got hold of the idea and are seeking to prove our nascent desire for national life on the strength of this new-found theory of theirs….

"…. Each thing in this world has two facets to it; and so there are two facets also to the clash and conflict that we meet with in our lives. It is the disharmony of these conflicts which arrests our attention and the deeper harmony that lies beyond is unheard by us. Thus the war that is ravaging Europe at the present day seems altogether evil and terrible to outer view…. And even so, Europe is stepping onwards to a larger harmony and peace, through the pain, misery and starvation of to-day; and when the fire of this war is quenched, you will find that Europe has outgrown that terrible pre-occupation with self which is the besetting feature of its energies at the present moment, I cannot deny that this war is the consequence of nationalism pushed to its excess; but the larger union among the peoples of Europe is bound to come its consequence of this war—who will deny that this too will be the fruit of the same principle of nationalism?

".... There is another point which requires consideration along with what I have said above. We say often that the advent of the British people was in accordance with a Divine dispensation, and this is what my friend S.P. Sinha reported in his presidential address at Bombay. We speak much also in the same connection about the union between the East and the West. These two points are at bottom one and the same and they require to be considered together.

"Kipling has said: 'The West is West and the East is East, and never the twain shall meet'. On the other hand there are people both here and in England, according to whom the union between East and West is inevitable, is bound to come. Sir Rabindranath has said in America that a universal brotherhood of mankind will replace the modern divisions among races and nationalities, and Sir S.P. Sinha spoke thus in Bombay: 'The East and West have met—not in vain. The invisible scribe, who has been writing the most marvellous history that has ever been written, has not been idle. Those who have the discernment and inner vision to see will note that there is one goal, one path.'

"The more I think of these opposite poles of opinion the more I believe that they are both true and both false. Let us consider what the importance of this union between the East and the West may be; and for the purpose of argument let us take England as typical of the West and Bengal as typical of the East. If by the union of Bengal and England it is meant that Bengal will be a sort of mimic England and that we the Bengalis will be mimic Englishmen and Englishwomen; if it is meant that our education, agriculture and trade will be anglicised and that this country instead of being a peaceful, domestic hermitage will develop into some huge and gigantic factory—then I say that such union is absolutely impossible. There are some who will object: Why should it be impossible? There are many even in this town who mould their lives entirely upon English lines and who live, dress and dine like Europeans. Also, the trade and industry of Calcutta are cast entirely upon English models; and the fashion of Calcutta easily and naturally becomes diffused over the rest of the province. How then can it be said that we shall not grow up altogether after a European pattern? My answer would be that it is easy to imitate a foreign thing but difficult to grow up into the genius of that foreign thing.... Now, I can never bring myself to believe that the gerto or organism of English civilization is implanted in the nature and constitution of Bengal, and hence I think that it is impossible that the Bengali will ever grow into the genius and civilization of England. Considered from this point of view, it seems that Kipling is right, that the East will always be East and the West will always be West and permanent union between the two must be forever unattainable.

"Then, again, will it be said that union between the East and the West will mean that both will lose their individual peculiarities and that each, by admixture with the other, will grow into a curious and hybrid product different from its native and natural genius? Such an opinion is so utterly at variance with the reality of things that it does not deserve serious consideration.

"There are others again who put a curious interpretation upon this union between the East and the West. They say that we shall adopt what is best in the West and that the West will adopt what is best in the East and a curious amalgam—a composite nationality—will thus be the result.... The elements of good and evil do not exist separately either in us or in the character of the English. Rather, these elements are inextricably intertwined and rooted deep in the fundamentals of national character so that it is impossible to leave out the bad and accept the good alone.... If we want to reform our national character, we must do so with the help of the forces which are latent in our own national individuality. The forces of European social life will be powerless and unavailing for that. Just as no permanent union can be effected by gluing together two separate physical things so no permanent union can be effected by improving special features from the life of a foreign nationality and seeking to graft them upon the genius and character of our own nation. In nations as in individuals we meet, not with the operation of mechanical forces, but with the play of life; and life will never develop into any form the seed of which is not inherent in itself.

".... But though there will be no fusion between the East and the West and no mechanical or electric union between them, yet I, together, with many others, believe in the possibility of a deeper union between these two entities. Now, what will be the nature of this union? This question may be considered from two points—the point of view of nationality and the point of view of government and administration,—considered from the second standpoint, it may be said that the Bengalis and the English will both preserve the distinctive type of their national character, yet, in affairs of higher administration and government, there is bound to come about an ultimate union between the two. What the precise character of the administrative union between England and India may be, it will be impossible to forecast from now. In his presidential address at the Bombay National Congress, Sir S.P. Sinha said:—'It seems to me that having fixed our good it is hardly necessary to attempt to define in concrete terms the precise relationship that will exist between England and India when the goal is reached.' Such also is my opinion. Only I should like to add that the relation that will be ultimately established between England and India will be such that it will not destroy the national individuality of either.

"If we consider the questions now from the standpoint of nationality, the ground of permanent union between England and India will be at once apparent. I have said already that union between two nationalities becomes possible only when each has reached its fullest point of development. Hence, there will be permanent union between England and Bengal only when each has developed the highest perfection that is open and possible unto it. True union does not lead to fusion or the complete merging of one in another; rather it leads to the complete development of the distinctive type and character which is latent in each separate factor. Distinctiveness can never be abolished; nationality can never perish. Union only brings into clear prominence the deeper harmony which underlies all outer differences between different nationalities. The universal brotherhood of man is possible only here; and only from this point of view it can be said that the East and West have met and not in vain.

"To sum up what I have said before: In order to advance the true welfare of our country, we shall have to look to our newly awakened national life; we shall have to look to the continuity of our national history;

we shall have to consider our actual present condition; and then we shall have to adopt such measures for the improvement of those conditions as may be consonant with our national life and the continuity of our national history" (Ghosh· 1972).

Chittaranjan further elaborated on the present condition of the country, its education system, the various causes of failures even after adopting the measures for expansion and the responsibilities that one needs to uphold in order to develop the country. He summarised his views by saying,

"1. We must give heed to the lessons of history.
2. We must abandon the path of European industrialism.
3. We must stop the decay of villages and the consequent congestion of cities.
4. To do this we shall have to rehabilitate our villages.
5. But our villages can only be rehabilitated if we make them sanitary, and thus enable the peasant to pursue his avocations free from disease.
6. We must train up the agriculturist in the ways of useful handicrafts.
7. We must enquire into the commercial and industrial products of Bengal in the past.
8. We must start small business concerns all over the country with a view to producing those articles for which our people have natural aptitude and skill.
9. We must stop importing foreign commercial products except such as are absolutely essential.
10. We must provide cheap capital for such industries as have a reasonable chance of

> being profitable, and with this end in view, we must start banking institutions in the different districts."

Chittaranjan painted a picture of Bengal, as beautifully as one could and reminded the people of how they could improve the condition of the whole country by taking the example from the glorious past of Bengal and by participating actively in all the aspects of development, like earlier times.

This speech bore witness to how Chittaranjan was becoming more of a political leader with the sound mind of a brilliant lawyer who could win an argument with anybody, on the basis of the facts that he presented with such affection for his country.

Soon the Declaration of August 20, 1917, was made where the plans for constitutional reforms was put forth, which ultimately led the Montague-Clemsford Bill to be passed by the Government of India as an Act in 1919. These reforms allowed more Indians to enter the Parliament giving them more provisions. Although this Act was not accepted by the Indians at large, nevertheless, it was a huge step taken by the government.

❑

8

THE POLITICIAN

"We prefer self-government with danger to servitude in tranquillity" Kwame Nkrumah, the first Prime Minister and then the first President of Ghana, spoke these words for his countrymen who were under the British colonial rule for a very long time.

Abraham Lincoln had also said, in his speech on Kansas-Nebraska Act in October 1854, "I trust I understand, and truly estimate the right of self-government. My faith in the proposition that each man should do precisely as he pleases with all which is exclusively his own lies at the foundation of the sense of justice there is in me. I extend the principles to communities of men, as well as to individuals. I so extend it, because it is politically wise, as well as naturally just: politically wise, in saving us from broils about matters which do not concern us.... When the white man governs himself, and also governs *another* man, that is *more* than self-government; that is despotism."

These words which the two men spoke, although meant for entirely different matters, cannot be ignored. They seemed to fit the condition of India during the time when our leaders fought for *Swaraj*.

Everybody remembers these words spoken by Lokmanya Tilak, "Freedom is my birth right and I shall have it." He fought for *Swaraj* along with Chittaranjan Das and others and they were unfortunately tagged as the 'Extremists', although they themselves never claimed that they were a separate group.

"Obviously, freedom as the definition of a man does not depend upon others, but as soon as there is a commitment, I am obliged to will the liberty of others at the same time as my own. I cannot make liberty my aim unless I make that of others equally my aim.... Those who hide from this total freedom, in a guise of solemnity or with deterministic excuses, I shall call cowards. Others, who try to show that their existence is necessary, when it is merely an accident of the appearance of the human race on earth—I shall call scum."

These were harsh words, but nonetheless true. Jean Paul Sartre in his lecture given on *Existentialism is Humanism* in 1946, said these words about individual freedom. He expressed his thoughts about how freedom is the most essential right of a human being.

Thus, *Swaraj*, meaning self-governance is one of the basic rights of a country. If a country is not allowed to rule itself, then who is? How can anybody else have any right to rule oneself? It is one of the most basic and essential rights of any nation and thus, one cannot simply be allowed to take that right away from you.

It is thus, only logical when the freedom fighters of the nation tried to attain this right by all means. No amount of politics and schemes of the British could ever lead them into believing that they were helping their nation by handling their country's affairs.

"I want my liberty. I want my freedom. I want my right to establish our own system of government.... We must be the judges of what system of government is good for us and what system of government will not suit us. It is not for other people to constitute themselves as judges" (Grover, 1994).

These words of Chittaranjan Das, spoken at the All-India Swaraj Party Conference held in Calcutta in 1924, show that he 'knew' what he wanted.

From 1917, until his death, Chittaranjan assumed the role of a Freedom Fighter in the truest sense. He was a part of various movements but did everything on his own accord. If he followed Mahatma Gandhi, it was not without questioning his motives. He had his disagreements but his policy of fighting together was always in the forefront.

At the Calcutta Session of the Congress held in December 1917, Chittaranjan talked about the Resolutions for Self-Government. His exact words were,

"The ideal is firstly, Provincial Autonomy, viz., that the Government of India must have its sphere demarcated, its functions defined; all other functions should belong to the Provincial Governments of the particular province.... The functions of the Executive Government must be made subordinate to the Legislative Council which would represent the wishes of the people of the particular province.... That means that the Executive should be obedient to the Legislature. If they do not obey the commands of the Legislature we say we stop the supplies.... We have had enough of the Bureaucracy in this country. We have suffered and groaned under the misrule of 150 years, and not one day is to be lost in declaring our will and to see that our wishes are given effect to—that the powers which are in the hands of the

Bureaucracy today are transferred to the people of the country."

What did Chittaranjan demand for his nation? Self-rule, which was the right of his country. In doing so, how can anybody blame him of being an 'Extremist'? Who is an Extremist after all? The dictionary meaning of the word 'Extremist' is: one who violates common moral standards.

Chittaranjan had already expressed his irritation on this matter during the Hindu-Mohammedan Mass Meeting held in Calcutta in October the same year, where he even quoted *Statesman*, a newspaper which differentiated between the Extremists and Modernists.

If voicing one's opinion is violation of law, then probably he broke the law. But the basic human rights do not deny any human being from saying what he wants to. And thus, by that standard, he cannot be called an Extremist. His love for his country, his passion for Self-Governance, has nothing to do with Extremism.

In 1918, Chittaranjan gave a speech at the Town Hall criticising the Defence of India Act of 1915. In every session of the Congress, he tried to make people understand how the policies of the British were affecting their country and how important it was to set up their own government.

When the Jallianwallah Bagh massacre occurred in April 1919, Chittaranjan joined the Non-Official Enquiry Committee to find the truth behind General Dyer's orders. It was said that the General ordered his men to fire at the people in the meeting because he thought he was confronted by a revolutionary army.

"However we may dwell upon the difficulties of General Dyer during the Amritsar riots, upon the anxious and critical situation in the Punjab, upon the danger to Europeans throughout that province, upon the long delays which have taken place in reaching a decision about this officer, upon the procedure that was at this point or at that point adopted, however, we may dwell upon all this, one tremendous fact stands out—I mean the slaughter of nearly 400 persons and the wounding of probably three to four times as many, at the Jallianwallah Bagh on 13th April. That is an episode which appears to me to be without precedent or parallel in the modern history of the British Empire. It is an event of an entirely different order from any of those tragical occurrences which take place when troops are brought into collision with the civil population. It is an extraordinary event, a monstrous event, an event which stands in singular and sinister isolation.... These observations are mainly of a general character, but their relevance to the case under discussion can be well understood, and they lead me to the specific circumstances of the fusillade at the Jallianwallah Bagh. Let me marshall the facts. The crowd was unarmed, except with bludgeons. It was not attacking anybody or anything. It was holding a seditious meeting. When fire had been opened upon it to disperse it, it tried to run away. Pinned up in a narrow place considerably smaller than Traflagar Square, with hardly any exits, and packed together so that one bullet would drive through three or four bodies, the people ran madly this way and the other. When the fire was directed upon the centre, they ran to the sides. The fire was then directed to the sides. Many threw themselves down on the ground, the fire was then directed down on the ground. This was continued for 8 to 10 minutes, and it stopped only when the ammunition had reached the point of exhaustion."

This was a part of the statement given by Winston Churchill, the then Secretary of State for War, regarding the massacre at the House of Commons on July 8, 1920. It was thus natural for any Indian to be infuriated after knowing the full facts related to this event. What followed was therefore, inevitable.

At the Amritsar Conference of Congress in December 1919, Chittaranjan along with Lokmanya Tilak, criticised the Government of India Act of 1919 and called it inadequate and disappointing.

Also, at a meeting in Calcutta, he opposed the Rowlatt Act, which was passed by the British Government on March 10, 1919, in order to extend the emergency measures which were affective during the First World War. He did this by supporting Mahatma Gandhi's Passive Resistance or in other terms, Non-Cooperation Movement.

❑

9

THE NON-COOPERATION MOVEMENT

What is non-cooperation? Why was it important for India? These questions were answered by Mahatma Gandhi on March 12, 1920, when he addressed a crowd of about fifty thousand people in Madras at the South Beach near Presidency College. A part of his speech is given here:

"What is this non-co-operation, about which you have heard so much, and why do we want to offer this non-co-operation? I wish to go for the time being into the why. Here are two things before this country: the first and the foremost is the Khilafat question. On this the heart of the Mussalmans of India has become lacerated. British pledges given after the greatest deliberation by the Prime Minister of England in the name of the English nation have been dragged into the mire. The promises given to Moslem India on the strength of which, the consideration that was expected by the British nation was exacted have been broken, and the great religion of Islam has been placed in danger. The Mussalmans hold—and I venture to think they rightly hold—that so long as British promises remain unfulfilled, so long it is impossible for them to tender whole-hearted fidelity and loyalty to the British connection; and if it is to be a choice for a devout Mussalman between loyalty to the British connection and loyalty to his Code and Prophet, he will not require a second to make his choice,—and he has declared his choice. The Mussalmans say frankly openly and honourably to the whole world that if the British Ministers and the British nation do not fulfil the pledges given to them and do not wish to regard with respect the sentiments of 70 million of the inhabitants of India who profess the faith of Islam, it will be impossible for them to retain Islamic loyalty. It is a question, then for the rest of the Indian population to consider whether they want to perform a neighbourly duty by their Mussalman countrymen, and if they do, they have an opportunity of a lifetime which will not occur for another hundred years, to show their good-will, fellowship and friendship and to prove what they have been saying for all these long years that the Mussalman is the brother of the Hindu. If the Hindu regards that before the connection with the British nation comes his natural connection with his Moslem brother, then I say to you that if you find that the Moslem claim is just, that it is based upon real sentiment, and that at its back ground is this great religious feeling, you cannot do otherwise than help the Mussalman through and through, so long as their cause remains just, and the means for attaining the end remains equally just, honourable and free from harm to India. These are the plain conditions which the Indian Mussalmans have accepted; and it was when they saw that they could accept the proffered aid of the Hindus, that they could always justify the cause and the means before the whole world, that they decided to accept the proffered hand of fellowship. It is then for the Hindus and Mahomedans to offer a united front to the whole of the Christian powers of Europe and tell them that weak as India is, India has still got the capacity of preserving her self-respect, she still knows how to die for her religion and for her self-respect.

"That is the Khilafat in a nut-shell; but you have also got the Punjab. The Punjab has wounded the heart of India as no other question has for the past century. I do not exclude from my calculation the Mutiny of 1857. Whatever hardships India had to suffer during the Mutiny, the insult that was attempted to be offered to her during the passage of the Rowlatt legislation and that which was offered after its passage were unparalleled in Indian history. It is because you want justice from the British nation in connection with the Punjab atrocities: you have to devise, ways and means as to how you can get this justice. The House of Commons, the House of Lords, Mr. Montagu, the Viceroy of India, everyone of them know what the feeling of India is on this Khilafat question and on that of the Punjab; the debates in both the Houses of Parliament, the action of Mr. Montagu and that of the Viceroy have demonstrated to you completely that they are not willing to give the justice which is India's due and which she demands. I suggest that our leaders have got to find a way out of this great difficulty and unless we have made ourselves even with the British rulers in India and unless we have gained a measure of self-respect at the hands of the British rulers in India, no connection, and no friendly intercourse is possible between them and ourselves. I, therefore, venture to suggest this beautiful and unanswerable method of non-co-operation.

"I have been told that non-co-operation is unconstitutional. I venture to deny that it is unconstitutional. On the contrary, I hold that non-co-operation is a just and religious doctrine; it is the inherent right of every human being and it is perfectly constitutional. A great lover of the British Empire has said that under the British constitution even a successful rebellion is perfectly constitutional and he quotes historical instances, which I cannot deny, in support of his claim. I do not claim any constitutionality for a rebellion successful or otherwise, so long as that rebellion means in the ordinary sense of the term, what it does mean namely wresting justice by violent means. On the contrary, I have said it repeatedly to my countrymen that violence whatever end it may serve in Europe, will never serve us in India. My brother and friend Shaukat Ali believes in methods of violence; and if it was in his power to draw the sword against the British Empire, I know that he has got the courage of a man and he has got also the wisdom to see that he should offer that battle to the British Empire. But because he recognises as a true soldier that means of violence are not open to India, he sides with me accepting my humble assistance and pledges his word that so long as I am with him and so long as he believes in the doctrine, so long will he not harbour even the idea of violence against any single Englishman or any single man on earth. I am here to tell you that he has been as true as his word and has kept it religiously. I am here to bear witness that he has been following out this plan of non-violent non-co-operation to the very letter and I am asking India to follow this non-violent non-co-operation. I tell you that there is not a better soldier living in our ranks in British India than Shaukat Ali.... I believe that a man is the strongest soldier for daring to die unarmed with his breast bare before the enemy. So much for the non-violent part of non-co-operation. I therefore, venture to suggest to my learned countrymen that so long as the doctrine of non-co-operation remains non-violent, so long there is nothing unconstitutional in that doctrine.

"I ask further, is it unconstitutional for me to say to the British Government 'I refuse to serve you'? Is it unconstitutional for our worthy Chairman to return with every respect all the titles that he has ever held from the government? Is it unconstitutional for any parent to withdraw his children from a government or aided school? Is it unconstitutional for a lawyer to say 'I shall no longer support the arm of the law so long as that arm of law is used not to raise me but to debase me'? Is it unconstitutional for a civil servant or for a judge to say, 'I refuse to serve a government which does not wish to respect the wishes of the whole people'? I ask, is it unconstitutional for a policeman or for a soldier to tender his resignation when he knows that he is called to serve a government which traduces his own countrymen? Is it unconstitutional for me to go to the 'kisan,' to the agriculturist, and say to him 'it is not wise for you to pay any taxes if these taxes are used by the government not to raise you but to weaken you'? I hold and I venture to submit that there is nothing unconstitutional in it. What is more, I have done every one of these things in my life and nobody has questioned the constitutional character of it. I was in Kaira working in the midst of 7 lakhs of agriculturists. They had all suspended the payment of taxes and the whole of India was one with me. Nobody considered that it was unconstitutional. I submit that in the whole plan of non-co-operation, there is nothing unconstitutional. But I do venture to suggest that it will be highly unconstitutional in the midst of this unconstitutional government,—in the midst of a nation which has built up its magnificent constitution,—for the people of India to become weak and to crawl on their belly—it will be highly unconstitutional for the people of India to pocket every insult that is offered to them; it is highly unconstitutional for the 70 million of Mohamedans of India to submit to a violent wrong done to their religion; it is highly unconstitutional for the whole of India to sit still and co-operate with an unjust government which has trodden under its feet the honour of the Punjab. I say to my countrymen so long as you have a sense of honour and so long as you wish to remain the descendants and defenders of the noble traditions that have been handed to you for generations after generations, it is unconstitutional for you not to non-co-operate and unconstitutional for you to co-operate with a government which has become so unjust as our government has become. I am not anti-English; I am not anti-British; I am not anti any government; but I am anti-untruth—anti-humbug and anti-injustice. So long as the government spells injustice, it may regard me as its enemy, implacable enemy. I had hoped at the Congress at Amritsar—I am speaking God's truth before you—when I pleaded on bended knees before some of you for co-operation with the government. I had full hope that the British ministers who are wise, as a rule, would placate the Mussalman's sentiment that they would do full justice in the matter of the Punjab atrocities; and therefore, I said:—'let us return good-will to the hand of fellowship that has been extended to us', which I then believed was extended to us through the Royal Proclamation. It was on that account that I pleaded for co-operation. But to-day that faith having gone and obliterated by the acts of the British ministers, I am here to plead not for futile obstruction in the Legislative council but for real substantial non-co-operation which would paralyse the mightiest government on earth. That is what I stand for to-day. Until we have wrung justice, and until we have wrung our self-respect from unwilling hands and from unwilling pens there can be no co-operation. Our *Shastras* say and I say so with the greatest deference to all the greatest religious preceptors of India but without fear of contradiction, that our *Shastras* teach us that there shall be no co-operation between injustice and justice, between an unjust man and a justice-loving man, between truth and untruth. Co-operation is a duty only so long as government protects your honour, and non-co-operation is an equal duty when the government instead of protecting robs you of your honour. That is the doctrine of non-co-operation.

"I have been told that I should have waited for the declaration of the special Congress which is the mouth piece of the whole nation. I know that it is the mouthpiece of the whole nation. If it was for me, individual Gandhi, to wait, I would have waited for eternity. But I had in my hands a sacred trust. I was advising my Mussalman countrymen and for the time being I hold their honour in my hands. I dare not ask them to wait for any verdict but the verdict of their own Conscience. Do you suppose that Mussalmans can eat their own words, can withdraw from the honourable position they have taken up? If perchance—and God forbid that it should happen—the Special Congress decides against them, I would still advise my countrymen the Mussalmans to stand single handed and fight rather than yield to the attempted dishonour to their religion. It is therefore given to the Mussalmans to go to the Congress on bended knees and plead for support. But support or no support, it was not possible for them to wait for the Congress to give them the lead. They had to choose between futile violence, drawing of the naked sword and peaceful non-violent but effective non-co-operation, and they have made their choice. I venture further to say to you that if there is any body of men who feel as I do, the sacred character of non-co-operation, it is for you and me not to wait for the Congress but to act and to make it impossible for the Congress to give any other verdict. After all what is the Congress? The Congress is the collected voice of individuals who form it, and if the individuals go to the Congress with a united voice that will be the verdict you will gain from the Congress. But if we go to the Congress with no opinion because we have none or because we are afraid to express it, then naturally we wait the verdict of the Congress. To those who are unable to make up their mind I say by all means wait. But for those who have seen the clear light as they see the lights in front of them, for them to wait is a sin. The Congress does not expect you to wait but it expects you to act so that the Congress can gauge properly the national feeling. So much for the Congress.

"Among the details of non-co-operation I have placed in the foremost rank the boycott of the councils. Friends have quarrelled with me for the use of the word boycott, because I have disapproved—as I disapprove even now—boycott of British goods or any goods for that matter. But there, boycott has its own meaning and here boycott has its own meaning. I not only do not disapprove but approve of the boycott of the councils that are going to be formed next year. And why do I do it? The people—the masses,—require from us, the leaders, a clear lead. They do not want any equivocation from us. The suggestion that we should seek election and then refuse to take the oath of allegiance would only make the nation distrust the leaders. It is not a clear lead to the nation. So I say to you, my countrymen, not to fall into this trap. We shall sell our country by adopting the method of seeking election and then not taking the oath of allegiance. We may find it difficult, and I frankly confess to you that I have not that trust in so many Indians making that declaration and standing by it. To-day I suggest to those who honestly hold the view—that we should seek election and then refuse to take the oath of allegiance—I suggest to them that they will fall into a trap which they are preparing for themselves and for the nation. That is my view. I hold that if we want to give the nation the clearest possible lead, and if we want not to play with this great nation we must make it clear to this nation that we cannot take any favours, no matter how great they may be so long as those favours are accompanied by an injustice a double wrong, done to India not yet redressed. The first indispensable thing before we can receive any favours from them is that they should redress this double wrong. There is a Greek proverb which used to say 'Beware of the Greek but especially beware of them when they bring gifts to you.' To-day from those ministers who are bent upon perpetuating the wrong to Islam and to the Punjab, I say we cannot accept gifts but we should be doubly careful lest we may not fall into the trap that they may have devised. I therefore suggest that we must not coquet with the council and must not have anything whatsoever to do with them. I am told that if we, who represent the national sentiment do not seek election, the Moderates who do not represent that sentiment will. I do not agree. I do not know what the Moderates represent and I do not know what the Nationalists represent. I know that there are good sheep and black sheep amongst the Moderates. I know that there are good sheep and black sheep amongst the Nationalists. I know that many Moderates hold honestly the view that it is a sin to resort to non-co-operation. I respectfully agree to differ from them. I do say to them also that they will fall into a trap which they will have devised if they seek election. But that does not affect my situation. If I feel in my heart of hearts that I ought not to go to the councils I ought at least to abide by this decision and it does not matter if ninety-nine other countrymen seek election. That is the only way in which public work can be done, and public opinion can be built. That is the only way in which reforms can be achieved and religion can be conserved. If it is a question of religious honour, whether I am one or among many I must stand upon my doctrine. Even if I should die in the attempt, it is worth dying for, than that I should live and deny my own doctrine. I suggest that it will be wrong on the part of any one to seek election to these Councils. If once we feel that we cannot co-operate with this government, we have to commence from the top. We are the natural leaders of the people and we have acquired the right and the power to go to the nation and speak to it with the voice of non-co-operation. I therefore do suggest that it is inconsistent with non-co-operation to seek election to the Councils on any terms whatsoever.

"I have suggested another difficult matter, that the lawyers should suspend their practice. How should I do otherwise knowing so well how the government had always been able to retain this power through the instrumentality of lawyers. It is perfectly true that it is the lawyers of to-day who are leading us, who are fighting the country's battles, but when it comes to a matter of action against the government, when it comes to a matter of paralysing the activity of the government I know that the government always look to the lawyers, however fine fighters they may have been to preserve their dignity and their self-respect. I therefore suggest to my lawyer friends that it is their duty to suspend their practice and to show to the government that they will no longer retain their offices, because lawyers are considered to be honorary officers of the courts and therefore subject to their disciplinary jurisdiction. They must no longer retain these honorary offices if they want to withdraw on operation from government. But what will happen to law and order? We shall evolve law and order through the instrumentality of these very lawyers. We shall promote arbitration courts and dispense justice, pure, simple home-made justice, *swadeshi* justice to our countrymen. That is what suspension of practice means.

"I have suggested yet another difficulty—to withdraw our children from the government schools and to ask collegiate students to withdraw from the college and to empty government-aided schools. How could I do otherwise? I want to gauge the national sentiment. I want to know whether the Mahomodans feel deeply. If they feel deeply they will understand in the twinkling of an eye, that it is not right for them to receive schooling from a government in which they have lost all faith; and which they do not trust at all. How can I, if I do not want to help this government, receive any help from that government. I think that the schools and colleges are factories for making clerks and government servants. I would not help this great factory for manufacturing clerks and servants if I want to withdraw co-operation from that government. Look at it from any point of view you like. It is not possible for you to send your children to the schools and still believe in the doctrine of non-co-operation....

"Please remember that even in England the little children were withdrawn from the schools; and colleges in Cambridge and Oxford were closed. Lawyers had left their desks and were fighting in the trenches. I do not present to you the trenches but I do ask you to go through the sacrifice that the men, women and the brave lads of England went through. Remember that you are offering battle to a nation which is saturated with their spirit of sacrifice whenever the occasion arises. Remember that the little band of Boers offered stubborn resistance to a mighty nation. But their lawyers had left their desks. Their mothers had withdrawn their children from the schools and colleges and the children had become the volunteers of the nation, I have seen them with these naked eyes of mine. I am asking my countrymen in India to follow no other gospel than the gospel of self-sacrifice which precedes every battle. Whether you belong to the school of violence or non-violence you will still have to go through the fire of sacrifice, and of discipline."

Chittaranjan Das voiced similar thoughts on law and order and nationalism, when he spoke at the celebrated Gaya Conference later in December 1922. A part of his speech is given here:

"The truth is that law and order is for Man, and not Man for Law and Order. The development of nationality is a sacred task and anything which impedes that task is an obstacle which the very force and power of nationality must overcome. If, therefore, you interpose a doctrine to impede the task, why, the doctrine must go. If you have recourse to law and order to establish and defend the rule of law then your law and order is entitled to claim the respect of all law-abiding citizens; but as soon as you have recourse to it not to establish and defend of law but to destroy and attack it, there is no longer any obligation on us to respect it for Higher Law, the Law of God compels us to offer our stubborn resistance to it. When I find something put forward in the sacred name of law and order which is deliberately intended to hinder the growth, the development, and the self-realisation of the nation, I have no hesitation whatever in proclaiming that such law and order is an outrage on man and an insult to God.

"But though our Moderate friends are often deluded by the battle-cry of law and order, I rejoice when I hear that cry. It means that the Bureaucracy is in danger and that the Bureaucracy has realised its danger. It is not without reason that a false issue is raised; and the fact that false issue has been raised fills me with hope and courage.... Freedom has already advanced when the alarm of law and order is sounded that is the history of Bureaucracies all over the world....

"What is the ideal which we must set before us? The first and foremost is the ideal of nationalism.... It is, I conceive, a process through which a nation expressed itself and finds itself, not in isolation from other nations, not in opposition to other nations, but as part of a great scheme by which, in seeking its own expression and self-realisation of other nations as well.... The nationality of which I am speaking must not be confused with the conception of nationality as it exists in Europe today. Nationalism in Europe is an aggressive nationalism, a selfish nationalism, a commercial nationalism, of gain and loss.... I contend that each nationality constitutes a particular stream of the great unity, but no nation can fulfil itself unless and until it becomes itself and at the same time realises its identity with Humanity."

Chittaranjan was overwhelmed by Mahatma Gandhi and his thoughts on non-cooperation, and he left his practice in January 1921, at a time when he was earning around fifty thousand rupees a month.. He even initiated the boycott of foreign goods and his whole family started spinning and selling *khadi* in order to earn their living, now that he did not have any other source of revenue.

He had opposed this movement earlier at a Special Congress meeting in Calcutta on September 4, 1920, but when he met Gandhi, his doubts were cleared and he became an active member of the movement since December 1920, and declared it at the Nagpur session of the Congress.

Mrs. Mukerjea described her grandfather's sacrifice in these words,

"He had many European clothes and other things. But overnight, he gave up everything. When Mahatma Gandhi called out for Non-cooperation Movement, he started the boycott of foreign goods. He had met Gandhi and was greatly impressed by him. We only had *khadi* and he started wearing that and my entire family followed him. My mother had just got married. She had beautiful *sarees*; but she did not protest when he burnt them all. He was used to drinking good brandy, Napoleon Brandy. He even gave that up and all the Cuban cigars. He started smoking *hookah*. He wasn't against alcohol as such; but since he was boycotting everything foreign, he gave up all the imported ones....

"One day, he came home and said that he had resigned as a lawyer. So, she (my grandmother) just asked him then 'how are we going to live?' 'God will look after us', he replied. They all used to spin *khadi* and sell them to earn their livelihood."

Spinning *khadi* had become a kind of a phenomenon after the boycott of foreign clothes. It was for this reason that Basanti Devi was once arrested. She and Urmila Devi, one of Chittaranjan's sisters went to jail for selling *khadi*.

Chittaranjan's granddaughter recalls:

"My grandmother went to jail along with *pishima*. I asked my grandmother, what she did in the jail. She said, 'Both of us talked; we were in nearby cells so, we talked, although we couldn't touch each other.' A group of well-known citizens went to the governor and told him that they couldn't arrest a lady and then they were released. But my grandfather got very angry about it. He said they should have been kept in jail a little longer. This would have helped gain sympathy and help people listen to their cause for boycotting foreign goods. Even my father wanted his mother to be in jail a little longer."

The non-violent Non-cooperation Movement started by Mahatma Gandhi although a successful venture, had certain critic is as well. It was not possible to stop all aggressive activities all over the country and hence he called off the movement after hearing disturbing news of violence in certain pockets of the nation in March 1922. After this, Gandhi was imprisoned for six years on the charge of sedition.

❑

10

THE GAYA CONFERENCE

Chittaranjan kept himself quite busy even after leaving his practice at the High Court. He went on political tours in the eastern part of Bengal and Assam and even when he was refrained from entering Mymensingh, a district in Dacca, he disobeyed the prohibition order and visited Mymensingh and Tangrail. He established the National University in Dacca and also visited Habiganj, Maulvibazar, Sylhet, and Chittagong and attended the Barisal Conference of 1921.

Meanwhile, the Bengal Government declared that the formation of associations and volunteer groups was illegal and they banned all public meetings. The Congress and Khilafat Committee went against the government's decision and Chittaranjan was elected as the leader in Bengal. He issued manifestoes and asked lakhs of volunteers to join their movement but this too was declared as illegal by the government.

On December 6, 1922, Chiraranjan Das, Chittaranjan's son was arrested from Burrabazar, for volunteering in the movement. Mrs. Mukerjea talks about her father's imprisonment, "He died at 26, but went to jail three times himself. He said, 'how can my father ask others to join the movement, if his own son doesn't go to jail'. He died when I was 5 years old."

Next day, Chittaranjan's wife, Basanti Devi and sister, Urmila Devi, along with other ladies were arrested for selling *khadi*, but were released soon, much to the disappointment of Chittaranjan.

On December 10, Chittaranjan was arrested under the Criminal Law Amendment Act, Section 17B. He was then the elected President of the Congress for that year but could not attend the annual session because he was on trial (Ray, 1927).

The day when the Prince of Wales visited Calcutta, people of the city observed strike as they were observing non-violent non-cooperation.

From January 1922 to June 1922, Chittaranjan spent his time in jail. In July, when he was released, people of India rejoiced and in his honour, presented an address for him at Mirzapur Park.

In December the same year, the annual conference of the Congress was held at Gaya. Chittaranjan was presiding over it, and he gave a presidential speech.

One can really know everything about Chittaranjan Das through this speech which he gave at Gaya. Below is the Presidential Address of Chittaranjan at the thirty-seventh session of the Congress, which was held on December 26, 1922.

"As I stand before you to-day, a sense of overwhelming loss overtakes me, and I can scarcely give expression to what is uppermost in the minds of all and every one of us. After a memorable battle which he gave to the Bureaucracy, Mahatma Gandhi has been seized and cast into prison; and we shall not have his guidance in the proceedings of the Congress this year. But there is inspiration for all of us in the last stand which he made in the citadel of the enemy, in the last defiance which he hurled at the agents of the Bureaucracy. To read a story equal in pathos, in dignity, and in sublimity you have to go back over two thousand years, when Jesus of Nazareth, 'as one that perverted the people' stood to take his trial before a foreign tribunal.

"And Jesus stood before the Governor: and the Governor asked him saying, 'Art thou the king of the Jews?' And Jesus said unto him, 'Thou sayëst'.

"And when he has accused of the chief priests and elders, he answered nothing.

"Then said Pilate unto him, 'Hearest thou not how many things they witness against thee?'

"And he answered him to never a word; in so much that the Governor marvelled greatly.

"Mahatma Gandhi took a different course. He admitted that he was guilty, and he pointed out to the public Prosecutor, that his guilt was greater than he, the Prosecutor, had alleged; but he maintained that if he had offended against the law of Bureaucracy in so offending, he had obeyed the law of God. If I may hazard a guess, the Judge who tried him and who passed a sentence of imprisonment on him was filled with the same feeling of marvel as Pontius Pilate had been.

"Great in taking decisions, great in executing them, Mahatma Gandhi was incomparably great in the last stand which he made on behalf of his country. He is undoubtedly one of the greatest men that the world has ever seen. The world hath need of him and if he is mocked and jeered at by 'the people of importance,' the 'people with a stake in the country'—Scribes and Pharisees of the days of Christ he will be gratefully remembered now and always by a nation which he led from victory to victory."

Chittaranjan spoke these words in honour of

Mahatma Gandhi, who was imprisoned for six years in March 1922. He was trying to move the nation into following Gandhi's path by narrating the story of Jesus Christ. Later, Chittaranjan talked about the relevance of law and order in the governance of the country.

"Gentlemen, the time is a critical one and it is important to seize upon the real issue which divides the people from the Bureaucracy and its Indian allies. During the period of repression which began about this time last year, it was this issue which pressed itself on our attention. This policy of repression was supported and in some cases instigated by the Moderate Leaders who are in the Executive Government. I do not charge those who supported the government with dishonesty or want of patriotism. I say they were led away by the battle cry of law and order. And it is because I believe that there is a fundamental confusion of thought behind this attitude of mind that I propose to discuss this plea of law and order. 'Law and Order' has indeed been the last refuge of Bureaucracies all over the world.

"It has been gravely asserted not only by the Bureaucracy but also by its apologists, the Moderate Party, that a settled government is the first necessity of any people and that the subject has no right to present his grievances except in a constitutional way, by which I understand in some way recognised by the constitution. If you cannot actively co-operate in the maintenance of 'the law of the land' they say, 'it is your duty as a responsible citizen to obey it passively. Non-resistance is the least that the government is entitled to expect from you.'

"This is the whole political philosophy of the Bureaucracy—the maintenance of law and order on the part of the government, and an attitude of passive obedience and non-resistance on the part of the subject. But was not that the political philosophy of every English King from William the Conqueror to James II? And was not that the political philosophy of the Romanoffs, the Hohenzollerns and of the Bourbons? And yet freedom has come, where it has come, by disobedience of the very laws which were proclaimed in the name of law and order. Where the government is arbitrary and despotic and the fundamental rights of the people are not recognised, it is idle to talk of law and order....

".... I desire to emphasise one point and that is that throughout the long and bitter struggle between the Stuarts and Parliament, the Stuarts acted for the maintenance of law and order, and there is no doubt that both law and history were on their side....

".... The Revolution of 1688—a bloodless revolution—secured for England that Rule of Law which is the only sure foundation for the maintenance of law and order. It completed the work which the Long Parliament had begun and which the execution of Charles I had interrupted. But how was the peaceful revolution of 1688 brought about? By defiance of authority and by rigid adherence to the principle that it is the inalienable right of the subject to resist the exercise by the executive of wide, arbitrary or discretionary powers of constraint.

"The principle for which the revolution of 1688 stood was triumphantly vindicated in the celebrated case of Dr. Sacheverell. In the course of a sermon which he had preached, he gave expression to the following sentiment. 'The grand security of our government and the very pillar upon which it stands is founded upon the steady belief of the subjects' obligation to an absolute and unconditional obedience to the supreme power in all things lawful and the utter illegality of resistance on any pretence whatsoever. This is the doctrine of passive obedience and non-resistance the doctrine of law and order, which is proclaimed to-day by every bureaucrat in the country, foreign or domestic and which is supposed to be the last word on the subjects' duty and government's rights. But mark how they solved the problem in England in 1710. The Commons impeached Dr. Sacheverell giving expression to a view so destructive of individual liberty and the Lords by a majority of votes found him guilty. The speeches delivered in the course of the trial are interesting. I desire to quote a few sentences from some of those speeches. Sir Joseph Jekyll in the course of his speech said, 'that as the Law is the only measure of the Princes' authority and the peoples' subjection, so the law derives its being and efficacy from common consent; and to place it on any other foundation than common consent is to take away the obligation.' This notion of common consent puts both prince and people under, to observe the laws.

"'My Lords, as the doctrine of unlimited non-resistance was impliedly renounced by the whole nation in the resolution, so diverse Acts of Parliament afterwards passed expressing their renunciation, ...and, therefore I shall only say that it can never be supposed that the laws were made to set up a despotic power to destroy themselves and to warrant subversion of a constitution of a government which they were designed to establish and defend.' Mr. Walpole put the whole argument in a nutshell when he said, 'the doctrine of unlimited, unconditional passive obedience was first invented to support arbitrary and despotic power and was never promoted or countenanced by any government that had not designs sometime or other of making use of it.' The argument against the doctrine of law and order could not be put more clearly or forcibly, for his argument comes to this: 'that the doctrine is not an honest one if law and order is the process by which absolution consolidates its powers and strengthens its hand.' I will make one more quotation and that is from the speech of Major-Gen. Stanhope. 'As to the doctrine itself of absolute non-resistance, it should seem needless to prove by argument that it is inconsistent with the law of reason, with the law of Nature and with the practice of all ages and countries.... And indeed one may appeal to the practice of all Churches and of all states and of all nations in the world, how they behaved themselves when they found their civil and religious constitutions invaded and oppressed by tyranny.'

".... The conclusion is irresistible that it is not by acquiescence in the doctrine of law and order that the English people have obtained the recognition of their fundamental rights. It follows from the survey that I have made firstly that no regulation is law unless it is based on the consent of the people; secondly where such consent is wanting the people are under no obligation to obey; thirdly, where such laws are not only not based on the consent of the people but profess to attack their fundamental rights the subjects are entitled to compel their withdrawal by force or insurrections; fourthly, that law and order is and has always been a plea for absolutism and lastly there can be neither law nor order before the real reign of law begins.

"I have dealt with the question at some length as the question is a vital one and there are many Moderates who still think that it is the duty of every loyal subject to assist the government in the maintenance of law and order. The personal liberty of every Indian to-day depends to a great extent on the exercise by persons in authority of wide, arbitrary or discretionary powers. Where such powers are allowed, the rule of law is denied. To find out the extent to which this exploded doctrine of law and order influences the minds of sober and learned men we have only to read the report of the committee appointed to examine the repressive laws. You will find in the report neither the vision of the patriot nor the wisdom of the statesman; but you will find an excessive worship of that much advertised but much misunderstood phrase 'Law and Order.' 'Why is Regulation III of 1818 to be amended and kept on the Statute Book?' Because for the protection of the frontiers of India and the fulfilment of the responsibility of the Government of India in relation to Indian States there must be some enactment to arm the executive with powers to restrict the movements and activities of certain persons, who though not coming within the scope of any criminal law have to be put under some measure of restraint. Why are the Indian Criminal Law Amendment Act, 1908 and the Prevention of Seditious Meetings Act, 1911 to be retained on the Statute Book? For the preservation of law and order? They little think these learned gentlemen responsible for the report that these Statutes, giving as they do to the Executive wide, arbitrary and discretionary powers of constraint, constitute a state of things wherein it is the duty of every individual to resist and to defy the tyranny of such lawless laws. These Statutes in themselves constitute a breach of law and order, for, law and order is the result of the rule of law; and where you deny the existence of the rule of law, you cannot turn round and say it is your duty as law-abiding citizens to obey the law.

"We have had abundance of this law and order during the last few years of our National History. The last affront delivered to the nation, was the promulgation of an executive order under the authority of the Criminal Law Amendment Act making the legitimate work of Congress Volunteers illegal and criminal. This was supported by our Moderate friends on the ground that it is the duty of the law-abiding subject to support the maintenance of law and order. The doctrine has travelled all the way from the shores of England. But may I ask—is there one argument advanced to-day by the Bureaucracy and its friends which was not advanced with equal clearness by the Stuarts? When the Stuarts arrogated to themselves a discretionary power of committing to prison all persons who were on any account obnoxious to the Court, they made the excuse that the power was necessary for the safety of the nation. And the power was resisted in England, not because it was never exercised for the safety of the nation, but because the existence of the power was inconsistent with the existence, at the same time of individual liberty. When the Stuarts claimed the right to legislate by proclamation and by the wide exercise of suspending and dispensing powers they did so, on the express ground that such legislation was necessary for public safety. That right was denied by the English nation, not because such legislation was not necessary for public safety but because such right could not co-exist with the fundamental right of the nation to legislate for itself. Is the power of the Governor-General to certify that the passage of a Bill is essential for safety or tranquillity or interest of British India, any different from the power claimed by the Stuarts? There is indeed a striking resemblance between the power conferred on the Governor-General and the Governors of the provinces and the powers claimed by the Tudors and the Stuarts. When the Stuarts claimed the right to raise revenue on their own initiative, they disclaimed any intention to exercise such right except 'when the good and safety of the kingdom in general is concerned and the whole kingdom is in danger.' That right was resisted in England, not because the revenues raised by them were not necessary for the good and safety of the kingdom, but because that right was inconsistent with the fundamental right of the people to pay such taxes only as were determined by the representatives of the people for the people. Is the power conferred on the Governor to certify that the expenditure provided for by a particular demand not assented to by the legislature is essential to the discharge of his responsibility for the subjects, any different from the power claimed by the Stuarts? It should be patent to everybody that we do not live under any history of England as proclaimed that it is idle to talk of the maintenance of law and order when large discretionary powers of constraint are vested in the executive. The manhood of England triumphantly resisted the pretensions of 'law and order.' If there is manhood in India to-day, India will successfully resist the same pretensions, advanced by the Indian Bureaucracy.

"I have quoted from English History at length, because the argument furnished by that history appeals to people who are frightened by popular movement into raising the cry of 'law and order.' Follow the lines laid down in that History. For myself, I oppose the pretensions of 'law and order' not on historical precedent, but on the ground that it is the inalienable right of every individual and of every nation to stand on truth and to offer a stubborn resistance to the promulgation of lawless laws. There was a law in the time of Christ which forbade the people from eating on the Sabbath, but allowed the priests to profane Sabbath. And how Christ dealt with the law is narrated in the New Testament.

"At that time Jesus went on the Sabbath day through the corn; and his disciples were an hungered, and began to pluck the ear of corn and to eat.

"But when the Pharisses saw it, they said unto him, Behold, thy disciples do that which is not lawful to do upon the Sabbath day.

"But he said unto them, have we not read what David did, when he was an hungered and they that were with him;

"How he entered into the House of God and did eat the shew bread, which was not lawful for him to eat, neither for them which were with him, but only for the priests?

"Or have we not read in the law, how that on the Sabbath days the priests in the temple profaned the Sabbath and are blameless?"

Chittaranjan explains the benefits and drawbacks of following the law and order prescribed by the government by giving examples from the Parliament of England dating way back to the 12th Century.

These lines below have been quoted before but they have been repeated here in order to understand this particular speech. Chittaranjan continued,

"The truth is that law and order is for man, and not man for law and order. The development of nationality is a sacred task and anything which impedes that task is an obstacle which the very force and power of nationality must overcome. If therefore you interpose a doctrine to impede the task why, the doctrine must go. If you have recourse to law and order to establish and defend the rule of law, then your law and order is entitled to claim the respect of all law-abiding citizens, but, as soon as you have recourse to it not to establish and defend the rule of law, but to destroy and attack it, there is no longer any obligation on us to respect it, for a Higher Law, the virtual law, the Law of God compels to offer our stubborn resistance to it. When I find something put forward in the sacred name of law and order that it is deliberately intended to hinder the growth, the development, and the self-realization of the nation, I have no hesitation whatever in proclaiming that such law and order is an outrage on man and an insult to God.

"But though our Moderate friends are often deluded by the battle cry of law and order, I rejoice when I hear that cry. It means that the Bureaucracy is in danger and that the Bureaucracy has realised its danger. It is not without reason that the false issue is raised and the fact a false issue has been raised fills me with hope and courage. I ask my countrymen to be patient and to press the charge. Freedom has already advanced when the alarm of law and order is sounded; that is the history of Bureaucracies all over the world."

After pointing out the fault of the British Government in pushing law and order to the forefront in order to scare the general public, Chittaranjan went on to explain what the word Nationalism means and what the ideal of the country is.

"In the meantime it is our duty to keep our ideal steadfast. We must not forget that we are on the eve of great changes, that world forces are working all around us and that the battle of freedom has yet to be won.

"What is the ideal which we must set before us? The first and foremost is the ideal of Nationalism. Now what is Nationalism? It is, I conceive, a process through which a nation expresses itself and finds itself, not in isolation from other nations but, as part of a great scheme by which, in seeking its own expression and therefore its own identity, it materially assists the self-expression and self-realization of other nations as well."

Chittaranjan explained in these simple words his idea of a perfect world. He wanted an identity for his country, which was not considerable to ask. He believed that every country had a right to live by itself and in doing so it learns how to survive on its own. It does not need others to rule over them in the pretence of protecting it from the so-called dangers of the world. He further explained,

"Diversity is as real as Unity. And in order that the unity of the world may be established it is essential that each nationality should proceed on its own lines and find fulfilment in self-expression and self-realisation. The nationality of which I am speaking must not be confused with the conception of nationality as it exists in Europe to-day. Nationalism in Europe is an aggressive nationalism, a selfish nationalism, a commercial nationalism of gain and loss. The gain of France is a loss of Germany, and the gain of Germany is a loss of France. Therefore, French nationalism is nurtured on the hatred of Germany and German nationalism is nurtured in the hatred of France. It is not yet realised that you cannot hurt Germany without hurting Humanity and in consequence hurting France; and that you cannot hurt France without hurting Humanity, and in consequence hurting Germany. That is European nationalism; that is not the nationalism of which I am speaking to you to-day. I contend that each nationality constitutes a particular stream of the great unity, but no nation can fulfil itself until it becomes itself and at the same time realises its identity with Humanity. The whole problem of nationalism is therefore to find that stream and to face the destiny. If you find the current and establish a continuity with the past, then the process of self-expression has begun, and nothing can stop the growth of nationality.

"Throughout the pages of Indian history, I find a great purpose unfolding itself. Movement after movement has swept over this vast country, apparently creating hostile forces, but in reality stimulating the vitality and moulding the life of the people into one great nationality. If the Aryans and the non-Aryans met, it was for the purpose of making one people out of them. Brahmanism with its great culture succeeded in binding the whole of India and was indeed a mighty unifying force. Buddhism with its protests against Brahmanism served the same great historical purposes and from Magadha to Taxila was one great Buddhistic empire which succeeded not only in broadening the basis of Indian unity, but in creating what is perhaps more important, the greater India beyond the Himalayas and beyond the seas, so much so that the sacred city where we have met may be regarded as a place of pilgrimage of millions and millions of people of Asiatic races. Then came the Mahomedans of diverse races, but with one culture which was their common heritage. For a time it looked as if there was a disintegrating force, an enemy to the growth of Indian nationalism, but the Mahomedans made their home in India, and, while they brought a new outlook and a wonderful vitality to the Indian life, with infinite wisdom, they did as little as possible to disturb the growth of life in the villages where India really lives. This new outlook was necessary for India: and if the two sister streams met, it was only to fulfil themselves and face the destiny of Indian history. Then came the English with their alien culture, their foreign methods, delivering a rude shock to this growing nationality; but the shock has only completed the unifying process so that the purpose of history is practically fulfilled.

"The great Indian nationality is in sight. It already stretches its hands across the Himalayas not only to Asia but to the whole of the world, not aggressively, but to demand its recognition, and to offer its contribution, I desire to emphasise that there is no hostility between the ideal of nationality and that of world-peace. Nationalism is the process through which alone will world-peace come. A full and unfettered growth of Nationalism is necessary for world-peace just as a full and unfettered growth of individuals is necessary for nationality. It is the conception of aggressive nationality in Europe that stands in the way of peace; but once the truth is grasped that it is not possible for a nation to inflict a loss on another nation without at the same time inflicting a loss on itself, the problem of Humanity is solved. The essential truth of nationality lies in this, that it is necessary for each nation to develop itself, express itself and realise itself, so that Humanity itself may develop itself, express itself and realise itself. It is my belief that this truth of nationality will endure, although for the moment, unmindful of the real issue, the nations are fighting amongst themselves and, if I am not mistaken, it is the very instinct of selfishness and self-preservation which will ultimately solve the problem, not the narrow and the mistaken selfishness of the present, but a selfishness universalized by intellect and transfigured by spirit, a selfishness that will bring home to the nations of the world that in the efforts to put down their neighbours lies their own ruin and suppression."

Such beautiful thoughts Chittaranjan had on the topic of imperialism that one can only be awed by it. Nations did enter into the World War and the reason was the desire for power and some nations did ruin themselves in this want of power. He understood this and projected the true face of India as a peaceful nation who did not believe in attacking anyone and just wanted to be left alone. Thus, he put forward his concept of Nationalism by defining Self-Rule or *Swaraj* and non-violent non-cooperation method in front of the crowd at Gaya in these words,

"We have, therefore, to foster the spirit of nationality. True development of the Indian nation must necessarily lie in the path of *Swaraj*. A question has often been asked as to what is *Swaraj*. *Swaraj* is indefinable and is not to be confused with any particular system of government. There is also the difference in the world between *Swarajya* and *Samrajya*. *Swaraj* is the natural expression of the national mind. The full outward expression of that mind covers, and must necessarily cover the whole life history of a nation. Yet it is true that *Swaraj* begins when the true development of a nation begins, because, as I have said, *Swaraj* is the expression of the national mind.

"The question of Nationalism, therefore, looked at from another point of view, is the same question as that of *Swaraj*. The question of all questions in India to-day is the attainment of *Swaraj*.

"I now come to the question of method. I have to repeat that it has been proved beyond any doubt that the method of non-violent non-co-operation is the only method which we must follow to secure a system of government which may in reality be the foundation of *Swaraj*. It is hardly necessary to discuss the philosophy of non-co-operation. I shall simply state the different view points from which this question may be discussed. From the national point of view the method of non-co-operation means the attempt of the nation to concentrate upon its own energy and to stand on its own strength. From the ethical point of view, non-co-operation means the method of self-purification, the withdrawal from that which is injurious to the development of the nation, and therefore to the good of humanity. From the spiritual point of view, *Swaraj* means that isolation which in the language of *Sadhana* is called *protyahar*—that withdrawal from the forces which are foreign to our nature—an isolation and withdrawal which is necessary in order to bring out from our hidden depths the soul of the nation in all her glory. I do not desire to labour the point, but from every conceivable point of view, the method of non-violent non-co-operation must be regarded as the true method of 'following in the path of *Swaraj*.'"

Chittaranjan then goes on to present his opinion on the criticism that some organisations in the country expressed on non-violence as the method to attain *Swaraj*.

"Doubt has, however, been expressed in some quarters about the soundness of the principle of non-violence. I cannot refuse to acknowledge that there is a body of Indian opinion within the country as well as outside according to which non-violence is an ideal abstraction incapable of realisation, and that the only way in which *Swaraj* can ever be attained is by the application of force and violence. I do not for a moment question the sacrifice and patriotism of those who hold this view. I know that some of them have suffered for the cause which they believe to be true. But may I be permitted to point out that apart from any question of principle history has proved over and over again the utter futility of revolutions brought about by force and violence. I am one of those who hold to non-violence on principle. But let us consider the question of expediency. Is it possible to attain *Swaraj* by violent means? The answer which history gives is an emphatic 'No'. Take all the formidable revolutions of the world...."

He gave examples of French Revolution, revolutions in England and Russia and then continued with his view on this subject,

"I believe in revolutions, but I repeat, violence defeats freedom. The revolution of non-violence is slower but surer. Step by step the soul of the nation emerges and step by step the nation marches on in the path of *Swaraj*. The only method, by which Freedom can be attained in India at any rate, is the method of non-violent non-co-operation. Those who believe this method to be impracticable would do well to ponder over the Akali movement. When I saw the injuries of the wounded at Amritsar and heard from their lips that not one of them had even wished to meet violence by violence, in spite of such grave provocation, I said to myself, 'here was the triumph of non-violence.'

"Non-violence is not an idle dream. It was not in vain that Mahatma declared, 'put up thy sword into the sheath.' Let those who are 'of the truth' hear his voice as those others heard a mightier voice two thousand years ago.

"The attempt of the Indian nation to attain *Swaraj* by this method was, however, met by severe repression. The time has come for us to estimate our success as well as our failure. So far as repression is concerned, it is easy to answer the question. I have not the least doubt in my mind that the nation has triumphed over the repression which was started and continued to kill the soul of the movement.

"But the question, which agitates most minds, is as to whether we have succeeded in our work of non-violent non-co-operation. There is, I am sorry to say, a great deal of confusion of thought behind the question. It is assumed that a movement must either succeed or fail, whereas the truth is that human movements, I am speaking of genuine movements, neither altogether succeed nor altogether fail. Every genuine movement proceeds from an ideal, and the ideal is always higher than the achievement. Take the French Revolution. Was it a success? Was it a failure? To predicate either would be a gross historical blunder. Was the non-co-operation movement in India a success? Yes, a mighty success when we think of the desire for *Swaraj* which it has succeeded in awakening throughout the length and breadth of this vast country. It is a great success when we think of the practical result of such awakening, in the money which the nation contributed, in the enrolment of members of the Indian National Congress and in the boycott of foreign cloth. I go further and say that the practical achievement also consists of the loss of prestige suffered by Educational Institutions and the Courts of Law and the Reformed Councils throughout the country. If they are still resorted to, it is because of the weakness of our countrymen. The country has already expressed its strong desire to end these institutions. Yet it must be admitted that from another point of view, when we assess the measure of our success in the spirit of Arithmetic, we are face to face with 'the petty done' and 'the undone vast.' There is much which remains to be accomplished. Non-violence has to be more firmly established. The work of non-co-operation has to be strengthened, and the field of non-co-operation has to be extended. We must be firm but reasonable. The spirit of sacrifice has got to be further strengthened, and we must proceed with the work of destruction and creation more vigorously than before I say to our critics. I admit we have failed in many directions, but will you also not admit our success where we have succeeded?"

After proving the success of the non-violent non-cooperation movement, Chittaranjan spoke how Moderates and others blamed them for ruining the youth of the country and accused them of hypocrisy.

"We have been denounced by the Moderates for having corrupted the youth of this country. It has been asserted that we have taught sons to disobey their fathers, the pupils their teachers and the subjects the government. We plead guilty to the charge and we rely on every spiritual movement as argument in our support. Christ himself was tried for having corrupted the people and the answers which he gave in anticipation is as emphatic as it is instructive.

"'Think not that I am come to send peace on earth. I come not to send peace, but a sword.'

"'For I am come to set a man at variance against his father and the daughter-in-law against her mother-in-law.'

"It has been said that with love on our lips we have been preaching the Gospel of hatred. Never was such a vile slander uttered. It may be we have failed to love; it may be we lost ourselves some of us in hatred, but that only shows our weakness and imperfectness. Judge us by our ideals, not by what we have achieved. Wherever we have fallen short of our ideal, put it down to our weakness. On behalf of the Indian National Congress I deny the charge of hypocrisy. To those who are anxious to point out our defects, I say with all humility. 'My friends, if you are weak, come and join us and make us stronger. If the Leaders are worthless, come and join us to lead, and the leaders will stand aside. If you do not believe in the ideal what is the use of always criticising us in the light of that ideal?' We need no critic to tell us how far we have fallen short of that ideal. Evidence of weakness has met me from every direction which I have looked. But, in spite of our defects of human weakness, of human imperfection I feel bold enough to say that our victory is assured and that the Bureaucracy knows that our victory is assured.

"But though the method of non-violent non-co-operation is sure and certain, we have now to consider how best to apply that method to the existing circumstances of the country. I do not agree with those who think that the spirit of the nation is so dead that non-violent non-co-operation is no longer possible. I have given the matter my earnest thought and I desire to make it perfectly clear that there is absolutely no reason for entertaining any feelings of doubt or despair. The outward appearance of the people to-day is somewhat deceptive. They appear to be in a tired condition and a sense of fatigue has partially overcome them. But beneath all this exterior of quietude, the pulse of the nation beats as strongly as before and as hopefully as at the beginning of this movement. We have to consolidate the strength of the nation. We have to devise a plan of work which will stimulate their energy, so that we can accelerate our journey towards *Swaraj*. I shall place before you one by one the items of work which in my opinion the Indian National Congress should prescribe for the nation."

Chittaranjan then suggested that the Congress in the name of *Swaraj* should declare certain rights which would help in the peaceful co-existence of Hindus and Muslims. His exact words were,

"It should commence its work for the year, by a clearer declaration of rights of the different communities in India under the *Swaraj* Government. So far as the Hindus and Mahomedans are concerned, there should be a clear and emphatic confirmation of what is known as the Lucknow pact and along with that there should be an emphatic insistence of each others' rights. And each should be prepared to undergo some kind of sacrifice in favour of the other. Let me give an instant to make my meaning clear. Every devout Mussalman objects to any music in front of a mosque and every devout and orthodox Hindu objects to cows being slaughtered. May not the Hindus and Mussalmans of India enter into a solemn pact so that there may not be any music before any mosque and that no cows may be slaughtered? Other instances may be quoted. There should be a scheme of a series of sacrifices to be suffered by each community so that they may advance shoulder to shoulder in the path of *Swaraj*. As regards the other communities such as Sikhs, Christians and Parsees, the Hindus and Mohamedans who constitute the bulk of the people should be prepared to give them even more than their proportional share in the *Swaraj* administration, I suggest that the Congress should bring about real agreement between all these communities, by which the rights of every minority should be clearly recognised in order to remove all doubts which may arise and all apprehensions which probably exist. I need hardly add that I include among Christians not only pure Indians but also Anglo-Indians and other people who have chosen to make India their home. Such an agreement as I have indicated was always necessary but such an agreement is especially necessary in view of the work which faces us to-day."

The importance of foreign propaganda and the call for participation in Asiatic Federation were then explained by Chittaranjan to the crowd in these words,

"I further think that the policy of exclusiveness which we have been following during the last two years be now abandoned. There is in every country a number of people who are selfless followers of liberty and who desire to see every country free. We can no longer afford to lose their sympathy and co-operation. In my opinion there should be established Congress agencies in America and in every European country. We must keep ourselves in touch with the world's movements and be in constant communication with the lovers of freedom all over the world.

"Even more important than this is the participation of India in the great Asiatic Federation which I see in the course of formation. I have hardly any doubt that the Pan-Islamic movement which was started on a somewhat narrow basis has given way or is about to give way to the great Federation of all Asiatic people. It is the union of the oppressed nationalities of Asia. Is India to remain outside the union? I admit that our freedom must be won by ourselves, but such a bond of friendship and love of sympathy and co-operation between India and the rest of Asia, nay between India and all the liberty-loving people of the world is destined to bring about

World Peace. World Peace, to my mind, means the freedom of every nationality and I go further and say that no nation in the face of the earth can be really free when other nations are in bondage. The policy which we have hitherto pursued was absolutely necessary for the concentration of the work which we took upon ourselves to perform and I agreed to that policy whole-heartedly. The hope of the attainment of *Swaraj* or a substantial basis of *Swaraj* in the course of the year made such concentration absolutely necessary. To-day that very work demands broader sympathy and a wider outlook."

Chittaranjan then talks about the demands which need to be revised regarding *Khilafat, Swaraj* and the wrong which happened with Punjab.

"We are on the eve of great changes, and the world-forces are upon us. The victory of Kemal Pasha has broken the bonds of Asia and she is all astir with life. It is Prometheus who spoke within her, and 'her thoughts' are like the many forests of vale through which the might of whirlwind and rain had passed. The stir within every European country for the real freedom of the people has also worked a marvellous transformation in the mentality of subject races. That which was more or less a matter of Ideal has now come within the range of practical politics. The Indian nation has found out its bearings. At such a time as this it is necessary for us to reconsider and to restate our demands. Our demands regarding the Punjab wrongs have got to be restated because many of them have already been realised. Our demands regarding *Khilafat* have got to be reconsidered, because some of them have already been worked out and we hope that before Lausanne Commission has finished their work very little of it will remain unrealised. Our demand for *Swaraj* must now be presented in a more practical shape. The Congress should frame a clear scheme of what we mean by a system of government which may serve as a real foundation for *Swaraj*. Hitherto, we have not defined any such system of government. We have not done as advisedly as it was on the psychological aspect of *Swaraj* that we concentrated our attention. But circumstances to-day have changed. The desire is making us impatient. It is therefore the duty of the Congress to place before the country a clear scheme of the system of government which we demand. *Swaraj*, as I have said, is indefinable and is not to be confused with any particular system of government. Yet the national mind must express itself, and although the full outward expression of *Swaraj* covers the whole life history of a nation, the formulation of such a demand cannot be any further delayed."

Further, Chittaranjan points out the schemes the British Government were applying, which ultimately would not be of much help to the Indians at large. He also offers his own suggestions for the proper governance of the country.

"It is hardly within the province of this address to deal with any detail scheme of any such government. I cannot, however, allow this opportunity to pass without giving you an expression of my opinion as to the character of that system of government. No system of government which is not for the people and by the people can even be regarded as the true foundation of *Swaraj*. I am firmly convinced that a parliamentary government is not a government by the people and for the people. Many of us believe that the middle class must win *Swaraj* for the masses. I do not believe in the possibility of any class movement being ever converted into a movement for *Swaraj*. If to-day the British Parliament grants

Provincial Autonomy in the provinces with responsibility in the Central Government, I for one, will protest against, because that will inevitably lead to the concentration of the power in the hands of the middle class. I do not believe that the middle class will then part with their power. How will it profit India, if in place of the White Bureaucracy that now rules over her, there is substituted an Indian Bureaucracy of the middle classes. Bureaucracy is Bureaucracy and I believe that the very idea of *Swaraj* is inconsistent with the existence of a Bureaucracy. My ideal of *Swaraj* will never be satisfied unless the people co-operate with us in its attainment. Any other attempt will inevitably lead to what European Socialists call the 'Bourgeoise' Government. In France and in other European countries it is the middle class who fought the battle of freedom and the result is that power is still in the hands of this class. Having usurped the power they are unwilling to face with it. If to-day the whole Europe is engaged in a battle of real freedom it is because the nations of Europe are gathering their strength to wrest this power from the hands of the middle classes. I desire to avoid repetition of that chapter of European history. It is for India to show the light to the world, *Swaraj* by non-violence and *Swaraj* by the people.

"To me the organisation of village life and the practical autonomy of small local centres are more important than either provincial autonomy or central responsibility; and if the choice lay between the two, I would unhesitatingly accept the autonomy of the local centres. I must not be understood as implying that the village centres will be disconnected units. They must be held together by a system of co-operation and integration. For the present, there must be power in the hands of the provincial and the

Indian Government; but the ideal should be accepted once for all, that the proper function of the central authority, whether in the provincial or in the Indian Government is to advise, having a residuary power of control only in case of need and to be exercised under proper safeguard. I maintain that real *Swaraj* can only be attained by vesting the power of government in these local centres, and I suggest that the Congress should appoint a committee to draw up a scheme of government which would be acceptable to the nation.

"The most advanced thought of Europe is turning from the false individualism on which European culture and institutions are based to what I know to be the ideal of the ancient village organisation of India. According to this thought modern democracy of the ballot box and large crowds has failed, but real democracy has not yet been tried. What is the real democracy of modern European thought?

"The foundation of real democracy must be laid in small centres—not gradual decentralisation which implies a previous centralisation—but a gradual integration of the practically autonomous small centres into one living harmonious whole. What is wanted is a human state, not a mechanical contrivance. We want the growth of institutions and organisations which are really dynamic in their nature and not the mere static stability of a centralised state.

"This strain of European thought found some expression in the philosophy of Hegel according to whom 'human institutions belong to the region not of inert externality, but of mind and purpose and are therefore dynamic and self-developing.'

"Modern European thought has made it clear that from the individual to the 'unified state,' it is one continuous process of real and natural growth.

Sovereignity (*Swaraj*) is a relative notion. 'The individual is sovereign over himself'—attains his *Swaraj* 'insofar as he can develop control and unify his manifold nature.' From the individual we come to the integrated neighbourhood which is the real foundation of the unified state, which again in its turn gives us the true ideal of the world-state. This integrated neighbourhood is a great deal more than the mere physical contiguity of the people who live in the neighbourhood area. It requires the coalition of what has been called 'neighbourhood consciousness.' In other words, the question is 'how can the force generated by the neighbourhood life become part of our whole critic and national life?' It is this question which now democracy takes upon itself to solve.

"The process prescribed is the generation of the collective will. The democracy which obtains to-day rests on an attempt of securing a common will by a process of addition. This really means a war of wills, the issue being left to be decided by a mere superiority of numbers. New democracy discountenances this process of addition, and insists on the discovery of detailed means and methods by which the different wills of a neighbourhood entity may grow into one common collective will. This process is not a process addition but of integration and the consciousness of the neighbourhood thus awakened must express the common collective will of that neighbourhood entity. The collective will of several neighbourhood centres, must by a similar process of integration be allowed to evolve the common collective will of the whole nation. It is only thus, by a similar process of integration that any league of nations may be real and the vision of a world-state may be realized. The whole of this philosophy is based on the idea of the evolution of the individual. The idea is to 'release the powers of the individual.' Ordinary notions of state have little to do with true individualism, (i.e.) with the individual as consciously responsible for the life from which he draws his breath and to which he contributes his all. According to this school of thought 'Representative government, party organisation, majority rule, with all their excrescences in their stead must appear the organisation of non-partisan groups for the begetting, the bringing into being of common ideas, a common purpose and the collective will.' This means the true development and extension of the individual self. The institutions that exist to-day have made machines of men. No government will be successful, no true government is possible which does not rest on the individual. 'Up to the present moment,' says the gifted authoress of the New State, 'we have never seen the individual yet. The search for him has been the whole long striving of our Anglo-Saxon history. We sought to improve the method of representation and failed to find him. We sought to reach him by extending the suffrage to every man and then to every woman and yet he eludes us. Direct government now seeks the individual.' In another place the same writer says; 'Thus group organisation releases us from the domination of mere numbers, thus democracy transcends time and space. It can never be understood except as a spiritual force. Majority rule rests on numbers; democracy rests on the well-grounded assumption that society is not a collection of units, but a network of human relations. Democracy is not worked out at the polling booths, it is the bringing forth of a genuine collective will, one to which every single being must contribute the whole of his complex life, as one which every single being must express the whole of it at one point. Thus the essence of democracy is creating. The technique of democracy is group organization.' According to this school of thought no living state is possible without the development and the extension of the individual self. The state itself is no static unit. Nor is it an arbitrary creation. 'It is a process; a continual self-modification to express its different stages of growth in which each and all must be so flexible that continual change of form is twin fellow of continual growth.' This can only be realised when there is a clear perception that individuals and groups and the nation stand in no antithesis. The integration of all these into one conscious whole means and must necessarily mean the integration of the wills of individuals into the common and collective will of the entire nation.

"The general trend of European thought has not accepted the ideal of this new democracy. But the present problems which are agitating Europe seems to offer no other solution. I have very little doubt that this ideal which appears to many practical politicians as impracticable will be accepted as the real ideal at no distant future. 'There is little yet,' I again quote from the same author, 'that is practical in practical politics.'

"The fact is that all the progressive movements in Europe have suffered because of the want of a really spiritual basis and it is refreshing to find that this writer has seized upon it. So to those who think that the neighbourhood group is puny to serve as a real foundation of self-government, she says, 'is our daily life profane and only so far as we rise out of it do we approach the sacred life? Then no wonder politics are what they have become. But this is not the creed of men to-day; we believe in the sacredness of life; we believe that divinity is for ever incarnating in humanity, and so we believe in humanity and the common daily life of all men.'

"There is thus a great deal of correspondence between this view of life and the view which I have been endeavouring to place before my countrymen for the last 15 years. For the truth of all truths, is that the outer *leela* of God reveals itself in history. Individual Society, Nation, and Humanity are the different aspects of that very *leela* and no scheme of self-government which is practically true and which is really practical can be based on any other philosophy of life. It is the realisation of this truth which is the supreme necessity of the hour. This is the soul of Indian thought, and this is the ideal towards which the recent thought of Europe is slowly, but surely, advancing."

Encapsulating the suggestions which Chittaranjan mentioned above, he says,

"To frame such a scheme of government regard must therefore be had:—

1. To the formation of local centres more or less on the lines of the ancient village system of India.
2. The growth of larger and larger groups out of the integration of these village centres.
3. The unifying state should be the result of minor growth.
4. The village centres and the larger groups must be practically autonomous.
5. The residuary power of control must remain in the Central Government, but the exercise of such power should be exceptional and for that purpose proper safeguards should be provided, so that the practical autonomy of the local centres may be maintained and at the same time the growth of the Central Government

into a really unifying state may be possible. The ordinary work of such Central Government should be mainly advisory.

"As a necessary corollary to what I have ventured to suggest as the form of government which we should accept, I think that the work of organising these local centres should be forthwith commenced. The modern sub-divisions or even smaller units may be conveniently taken as the local centres, and larger centres may be conveniently formed. Once we have our local areas—'the neighbourhood group'—we should foster the habit of corporate thinking, and leave all local problems to be worked out by them. There is no reason why we should not start the government by these local centres to-day. They would depend for their authority on the voluntary co-operation of the people, and voluntary co-operation is much better than the compulsory co-operation which is at the bottom of the Bureaucratic rule in India. This is not the place to elaborate the scheme which I have in mind; but I think that it is essentially necessary to appoint a committee with power, not only to draw up a scheme of government but to suggest means by which the scheme can be put in operation at once."

Chittaranjan then gave his opinion on the issue of the Boycott of Councils at length. He expressed his disagreement on the subject of Mass Civil Disobedience as he thought that it does not serve any real purpose. He expressed his thoughts on this matter in the following words:

"The next item of work to which I desire to refer is the Boycott of Councils. Unhappily the question has become part of the controversy of Change or No change. To my mind the whole controversy proceeds on a somewhat erroneous assumption. The question is not so much as to whether there should be a change in the programme of the work; the real question is, whether it is not necessary now to change the direction of our activities in certain respects for the success of the very movement which we hold so dear. Let me illustrate what I mean. Take the Bardoli Resolution. In the matter of boycott of schools and colleges the Bardoli Resolution alters the direction of our activity, which does not in any way involve the abandonment of the boycott. During the *Swaraj* year the idea was to bring the students out of government schools and colleges, and if National schools were started they were regarded as concessions to the 'weakness' of those students. The idea was, to quote the words of Mahatma Gandhi, 'political' and not 'educational.' Under the Bardoli Resolution, however, it is the establishment of schools and colleges which must be the main activity of national education. The idea is 'educational' and if it still be the desire of the Congress to bring students out of government schools and colleges, it is by offering them educational advantages. Here the boycott of schools and colleges is still upheld, but the direction of our activities is changed. In fact, such changes must occur in every revolution, violent or non-violent, as it is only by such changes that the ideal is truly served.

"In the next place, we must keep in view the fact that according to the unanimous opinion of the members of the Enquiry Committee, Civil Disobedience on a large scale is out of question because the people are not prepared for it.

"I confess that I am not in favour of the restrictions which have been put upon the practical adoption of any system of civil disobedience, and in my opinion, the Congress should abolish those restrictions. I have not yet been able to understand why to enable a people to civilly disobey particular laws, it should be necessary that at least 80 per cent of them should be clad in pure 'Khadi'. I am not much in favour of general Mass Civil Disobedience. To my mind, the idea is impracticable. But the disobedience of particular laws which are eminently unlawful, laws which are the creatures of 'Law and Order,' laws which are like an outrage on humanity and an insult to God... disobedience of such laws is within the range of practical politics, and, in my opinion, every attempt should be made to offer disobedience to such laws. It is only by standing on truth that the cause of *Swaraj* may prevail. When we submit to such laws, we abandon the plank of truth. What hope is there for a nation so dead to the sense of truth as not to rebel against lawless laws, against regulations which insult their national being and hamper their national development?

"I am of opinion that the question of the boycott of Councils which is agitating the country so much must be considered and decided in the light of the circumstances I have just mentioned. There is no opposition in idea between such civil disobedience as I have mentioned and the entry into the Councils for the purpose and with the avowed object of either ending or mending them. I am not against the boycott of Councils. I am simply of opinion that the system of the Reformed Councils with their steel frame of the Indian Civil Service covered over by a diarchy of deadlocks and departments is absolutely unsuitable to the nature and genius of the Indian nation. It is an attempt of the British Parliament to force a foreign system upon the Indian people. India has unhesitatingly refused to recognise this foreign system as real foundation for *Swaraj*. With me, as I have often said, it is not a question of more or less;

I am always prepared to sacrifice much for a real basis of *Swaraj*, nor do I attach any importance to the question as to whether the attainment of full and complete independence will be a matter of 7 years or 10 years or 20 years. A few years is nothing in the life history of a nation. But I maintain India cannot accept a system such as this as a foundation of *Swaraj*. These Councils must therefore be either mended or ended. Hitherto we have been boycotting the Councils from outside. We have succeeded in doing much. The prestige of the Councils is diminished and the country knows that the people who adorn those chambers are not the true representatives of the people. But though we have succeeded in doing much, these Councils are still there. It shall be the duty of the Congress to boycott the Councils more effectively from within. Reformed councils are really a mask which the Bureaucracy has put on. I conceive it to be our clear duty to tear this mask from off their face. The very idea of boycott implies, to my mind, something more than mere withdrawal. The boycott of foreign goods means that such steps must be taken that these councils may not be there to impede the progress of *Swaraj*. The only successful boycott of these Councils is either to mend them in a manner suitable to the attainment of *Swaraj* or to end them completely. That is the way in which I advise the nation to boycott the Councils.

"A great deal of discussion has taken place in the country as to whether the boycott of Councils in the sense in which I mean it is within the principle of non-violent non co operation. I am emphatically of opinion that it does not offend against any principle of non-co-operation which has been adopted and applied by the Indian National Congress. I am not dealing with the logical or philosophical abstractions.

I am only dealing with that which the Congress has adopted and called non-co-operation. In the first place, may I point out that we have not up to now non-co-operated with the Bureaucracy? We have been merely preparing the people of this country to offer non-co-operation. Let me quote the Nagpur Resolution on non-co-operation in support of my proposition. I am quoting only the portions which are relevant to this point.

"Whereas in the opinion of the Congress the existing Government of India has forfeited the confidence of the country, and, whereas the people of India are now determined to establish Swaraj...now this Congress...declares that the entire or any part or parts of the scheme of non-violent non-co-operation with the renunciation of voluntary association with the present government at one end and the refusal to pay taxes at the other, should be put into force at a time to be determined by either the Indian National Congress, or the All-India Congress Committee and that 'in the meanwhile to prepare the country for it, effective steps should continue to be taken in that behalf.'

"Then follows the effective steps such as national education, boycott of law courts, boycott of foreign goods, etc., which must be taken 'in the meanwhile.' It is clear therefore that the Congress has not yet advocated the application of non-co-operation but has merely recommended certain steps to be taken so that at some time or other to be determined by the Congress, the Indian Nation may offer non-co-operation. In the second place, let us be judge of the character of this principle not by thinking of any logical idea or philosophical abstraction but by gathering principle from the work and the activity which the Congress has enjoined. When I survey the work it is clear to my mind that the Congress was engaged in a two-fold activity. In everything that the Congress has commanded there is an aspect of destruction as there is an aspect of creation. The boycott of lawyers and Law Courts means the destruction of existing legal institutions; and the formation of Panchayats means the creation of agencies through which justice may be administered. The boycott of schools and colleges means the destruction of the department of Education; and the establishment of National schools and colleges means the creation of educational institutions for the Youth of India. The boycott of foreign goods followed as it was by the burning of foreign goods coming into the country. But, on the other hand, the spinning wheel and looms means creative activity in supplying the people with indigenous cloth. Judged by this principle what is wrong about the desire either to convert the Councils into institutions which may lead us to *Swaraj*, or to destroy them altogether? The same two-fold aspect of creation and destruction is to be found in the boycott of Councils in the way I want them to be boycotted.

"It has also been suggested that it offends against the morality and spirituality of this movement. Let us take the two points separately. As regards morality apart from the ethics of non-co-operation, it has been urged that entering the Councils for the purpose of ending the Councils is unfair and dishonest. The argument implies that the Reformed Councils belong entirely to the Bureaucracy, and the idea is that we should not enter into other peoples' property with a view to injure it. To my mind, the argument is based on a misconception of facts. Inadequate as the Reforms undoubtedly are, I do not for a moment admit that the Reform Act was a gift of the British

Parliament. It was, to quote the words of Mahatma Gandhi, 'a concession to popular agitation.' The fact is that it is the resultant of two contending forces, the desire of the people for freedom and the desire of the Bureaucracy to oppose such a desire. The result is that it has travelled along lines neither entirely popular nor entirely bureaucratic. The people of India do not like these Reforms, but let us not forget that the Bureaucracy does not like them either because it is the result of two contending forces pulling in different directions or the Reforms have assumed a tortured state. But so far as the rights recognised are concerned, they are our rights—our property, and there is nothing immoral or unfair or dishonest in making use of the rights which the people have extorted from the British Parliament. If the fulfilments of the very forces which have succeeded in securing the Reforms require that the Councils should either be mended or ended, if the struggle for freedom compels the adoption of either course, what possible charge of immorality can be levelled against it? I admit if we had proposed to enter the Councils stealthily with the avowed object of co-operation keeping within our hearts the desire to break the Councils, such a course would undoubtedly have been dishonest. European diplomacy, let us hope, has been abolished by Indian National Congress under the leadership of Mahatma Gandhi. If we play now, we play with all our cards on the table.

"But some people say that it is immoral from the point of view of non-co-operation, because it involves an idea of destruction. The work of non-co-operation according to these,—I have the highest reverence for them,—is only to build our national life ignoring altogether the existence of the Bureaucracy. It may be an honest ideal, and, logically speaking, it may be the inner meaning of non-co-operation. But the non-co-operation which the Congress has followed is not so logical and I claim that if the principle of non-co-operation is to be advanced as a test of my programme, let it be the same principle which the Congress has accepted, adopted and applied. As I have already said, that principle countenance destruction as well as creation. As a matter of fact circumstanced as we are with Bureaucracy to the right and the Bureaucracy to the left Bureaucracy all around us, it is impossible to create without destroying: nor must it be forgotten that if we break, it is only that we may build.

"It has also been suggested that the very entry into the Council is inconsistent with the ideal of non-co-operation. I confess I do not understand the argument. Supposing the Congress had sanctioned an armed insurrection could it be argued that entry into the fort of the Bureaucracy is inconsistent with the principle of non-co-operation? Surely the charge of inconsistency must depend on the object of the entry. An advancing army does not co-operate with the enemy when it marches into the enemy's territory. Co-operation must therefore depend on the object with which such entry is made. The argument if analysed comes to this, that whenever the phrase entry into Councils is used it calls up the association of co-operation, and then the mere idea of this entry is proclaimed to be inconsistent with non-co-operation. But this is the familiar logical fallacy of our terms. Entry into the Councils to co-operate with the government and entry into the Councils to non-co-operate with the government are two terms and two different propositions....

"Next let us understand the opposition from the point of view of the spirituality of our movement. The question of spirituality is not to be confused with the dictates of any particular religion. I am not aware of the injunctions of any religion against entering the Councils with a view either to mend them or end them. I have heard from many Mahomedans that the Koran lays down no such injunction. Other Mahomedan friends have told me that there may be some difficulty on that ground, but that is a matter with regard to which I am not competent to speak. The *Khilafat* must answer that question with such assistance as they may obtain from the Ulemas. It is needless to point out that should the Ulemas come to the conclusion that under the present circumstances it would be an offence against their religion to enter the Councils; the Congress should unhesitatingly accept their decision because no work in this country towards the attainment of *Swaraj* is possible without the hearty co-operation of both Hindus and Mussalmans. But I am dealing with that spirituality which does not affect any particular creed or any particular religion. Judged from the standpoint of such spirituality what objection there can be in removing from our path by all legitimate means any obstacle to the attainment of *Swaraj*? We burned foreign cloth without a scruple, and the spirituality of the movement did not receive a shock when we burned them. It is as well to start with a clear conception as to what that spiritually is. Apart from any creedal or doctrinal injunction and apart from any question of morality, the basis of spirituality must be the attainment of freedom and of *Swaraj*. What is the duty which every human being owes not only to his race, not only to his nation, not only to humanity but also to his God? It is the right to fulfil oneself. It is the duty of living in the light of God. Shortly after my release from imprisonment I said in a public speech that all our national activities should be based on truth. Ever since that day questions and conundrums have been put to me. I have been asked to define what is truth. It has also been suggested that because I dare not tell the truth that I took refuge under the general expression. I still insist that our national activities must be based on truth. I repeat that I do not believe in politics, or in making water-tight compartments of our national life which is an indivisible organic whole. I repeat that as you cannot define life, you cannot define truth. The test of Truth is not logical definition. The test of Truth lies in its all-compelling force, in making itself felt. You know truth when you have felt it.... I look upon the attainment of freedom and *Swaraj* the only way of fulfilling oneself as individuals, as nations. I look upon all national activities as the real foundation of the service of that greater humanity which again is the revelation of God to man.... We have to fight against all corruptions and all immorality. It is only thus that freedom can be attained. Whatever obstacles there may be in the path of *Swaraj*, either of the individual or of the nation, or humanity at large, these obstacles must be removed by the individual if he desires his freedom by the nation, if that nation desires to ruin itself by all the nations of the world if the cause of humanity is to prosper. That being the spirituality of the movement as I understand it I am prepared to put away all obstacles that lic bctwccn the Indian nation and the attainment of its freedom, not stealthily but openly, reverently in the name of truth and God. Judged from this ideal of spirituality the entry into the Councils for the purpose I have stated is necessary to advance the cause of truth. Everything in connection with the controversy must be judged by that standard.

"At present the question before the country put by those members of the Civil Disobedience Enquiry Committee who are in favour of the Council Entry is simply that the members of the Congress should stand as candidates. It is unnecessary therefore to go into other questions raised such as in the matter of taking oath, the probability or otherwise of securing a majority and so on. With regard to the question of oath all that I need say at present is this that apart from the dictates of any particular religion which I do not propose to deal with, the question does not present any difficulty at all. The oath is a constitutional one. The king stands for the constitution. Great changes in the constitution have taken place in England under that very oath.... So far as the first point is concerned, there is nothing in my suggestion which militates against it. So far as the second point is concerned, I am aware that a forced interpretation has been sought to be put upon it, namely, that a member taking the oath is bound to discharge his duties faithfully to the Bureaucracy. All that I need say is, that there is no constitutional authority of any kind to justify that interpretation. To my mind the words mean a faithful discharge of a member's duties to his constituency by the exercise of powers recognised under the Reforms Act. I do not therefore understand what possible objection there may be to take the Oath. But there again the question does not arise at present.

"Various other questions have been asked as to whether it is possible to secure a majority and as to what we should do, supposing we are in a majority. I think it possible that having regard to the present circumstances of the country, the non-co-operators are likely to get the majority. I am aware of the difficulty of the franchise. I am aware of the rules which prevent many of us from entering the Councils; but making every allowances for all these difficulties, I believe that we shall be in the majority. But here also the question doesn't arise till we meet in the Congress of 1923 when the matter may be discussed not on suppositions but on actualities.

"As regards the question as to what we should do if we have the majority the answer is clear. We should begin our proceedings by a solemn declaration of the existence of our inherent right, and by formal demand for a constitution which would recognise and conserve those rights and give effect to our claims for the particular system of government which we may choose for ourselves. If our demands are accepted, then the fight is over. But, as I have often said, if it is conceded that we are entitled to have that form of government which we may choose for ourselves, and the real beginning is made with that particular form of government in view, then it matters nothing to me whether the complete surrender of power is made up to-day, or in five years or even in twenty years. If, however, our demand is not given effect to, we must non-co-operate with the Bureaucracy by opposing each and every work of the Council. We must disallow the entire Budget. We must move the adjournment of the House on every possible occasion and defeat every Bill that may be introduced. In fact we must so proceed that the Council will refuse to do any work unless and until our demands are satisfied. I am aware of the large powers of certification which Governors can exercise under the Reform Act. But government by certification is just as impossible as government by veto. Such procedure may be adopted on a few occasions. The time must soon come when the Bureaucracy must yield or withdraw the Reforms Act. In either case it is a distinct triumph for the nation, and either course if adopted by the Bureaucracy will bring us nearer to the realisation of our ideal.

"Another question is often asked, suppose we end these Reformed Councils,—what then? Could not the same question be asked with regard to every step the Congress has hitherto undertaken in the way of breaking, of destroying institutions. If we had succeeded in destroying the Educational Department, might not somebody ask—what then? If we had succeeded in destroying the legal institutions, might not the question be put with equal relevance? The fact is destruction itself will never bring us *Swaraj*. The fact further is that no construction is possible without destruction. We must not forget that it is not this activity or that activity by itself that can bring *Swaraj. It is the totality of our national activity in the way of destruction and in the way of creation that will bring Swaraj.* If we succeeded in demolishing these Reformed Councils you will find the whole nation astir with life. Let them put other obstacles in our way; we shall remove them with added strength and greater vitality.

"It has also been suggested that the Bureaucracy will never allow the non-co-operators to enter the Councils, they will alter the rules to prevent such entry. I cannot conceive of anything better calculated to strengthen the cause of non-co-operation than this. If any such rule is framed I should welcome it and again change the direction of our activity. The infant nation in India requires constant struggle for its growth and development. We must not forget that a great non-violent revolution is on the land, and we shall change the direction of our activities as often as circumstances require it. To-day the Councils are open and we must attack them,—to-morrow if the

Councils are closed, we must be prepared to deal with the contingency when it arises. What do we do when it pours with rain? We turn our umbrella in the direction from which the water comes. It is in the same way that we must turn the direction of our activities whenever the fulfilment of our national life demands it.

"The work of the Councils for the last two years has made it necessary for non-co-operators to enter the Councils. The Bureaucracy has received added strength from these Reformed Councils, and those who have entered the Councils, speaking generally, have practically helped the cause of Bureaucracy. What is most necessary to consider is the fact that taxation has increased by leaps and bounds. The expenditure of the Government of India has grown enormously since the pre-war year 1913-14.... The expenses of the current year are likely to be even higher. To meet the successive increases in expenditure, additional taxation was levied in 1916-17, 1917-18, 1919-20, 1921-22 and 1922-23. We may prepare ourselves for proposals for further additional taxation in the ensuing year. In spite of the levy of additional taxation, seven out of the last nine years have been years of deficit.

"The increase in military expenditure is chiefly responsible for the present financial situation.... As Sir Visveswaraya remarks the expenses under the head 'Civil Administration' also have shown a perpetual tendency to increase. As a part and parcel of the Reform Scheme, the emoluments of the members of the Indian Civil Service, the Indian Educational Service, the Indian Medical Service and of all the other services recruited in England have been enormously increased; and to maintain some kind of fairness the salaries of the subordinate services which are manned by Indians have also been increased.

"The financial situation in the provinces is not much better.... In the first year of the reform era, most of the provinces were faced with deficits and were just able to tide over their financial difficulties by drawing upon their balances. But in the current year, the financial situation in many of the provinces has become worse....

"I warn my countrymen against the policy of allowing these Reformed Councils to work their wicked will. There will undoubtedly be a further increase of taxation and there is an apprehension in my mind, I desire to express it with all the emphasis that I can command, that if we allow this policy of drift to continue the result will be that we shall lose the people who are with us to-day. Let us break the Councils if the Bureaucracy does not concede to the demands of the people. If there is fresh taxation as it is bound to be let the responsibility be on the Bureaucracy. Then you and I and the people will jointly fight the powers that be."

Chittaranjan then gives his view on the Labour Organisation. He says,

"I am further of opinion that the Congress should take up the work of Labour and Peasant organisation. With regard to labour there is a resolution of the Nagpur Congress, but I am sorry to say that it has not been acted upon. There is an apprehension in the minds of some non-co-operators that the cause of non-co-operation will suffer if we exploit labour for Congress purposes. I confess again I do not understand the argument. The word 'exploitation' has got an ugly association, and the argument assumes that labour and peasants are not with us in this struggle of *Swaraj*. I deny the assumption. My experience has convinced me that labour and the peasantry of India to-day are, if anything, more eager to attain *Swaraj* than the so-called middle and educated classes. If we are 'exploiting' boys of tender years and students of colleges, if we are exploiting the women of India, if we are exploiting the whole of the middle classes irrespective of their creed and caste and occupation, may I ask what justification is there for leaving out labourers and the peasants? I suppose the answer is that they are welcome to be the members of the Congress Committees but that there should not be a separate organisation of them. But labour has got a separate interest and they are often oppressed by foreign capitalists and the peasantry of India is often oppressed by a class of men who are the standard bearers of the Bureaucracy. Is the service of this special interest in any way antagonistic to the service of nationalism? To find bread for the poor, to secure justice to a class of people who are engaged in a particular trade or avocation—how is that work different from the work of attaining *Swaraj*? Anything which strengthens the national cause, anything which supports the masses of India is surely as much a matter of *Swaraj* as any other items of work which the Congress has in hand. My advice is that the Congress should lose no time in appointing a committee, a calm workable committee to organise labour, and the peasantry of India. We have delayed the matter already too long. If the Congress fails to do its duty, you may expect to find organisations set up in the country by labour and peasants detached from you, dissociated from the cause of *Swaraj* which will inevitably bring within the arena of a peaceful evolution class struggles and the war of special interests. If the object of the Congress be to avoid that disgraceful issue let us take labour and the peasantry in hand, and let us organise them both from the point of view of their own special interests and also from the point of view of the higher ideal which demands the satisfaction of their special interests and the devotion of such interests to the cause of *Swaraj*. Here again we have to make use of very selfishness of the labourers and peasants, as we know that the fulfilment of that very selfishness requires it's just and proper contribution to the life of the nation...."

Chittaranjan's boycott movement did not just involve burning of foreign clothes as was evident from his speech. He again explains to the people at Gaya what else he meant by destruction of foreign goods and creation of home-made products. He includes schools and colleges and the posts of lawyers and boycott of law courts. He says,

"...I am firmly of opinion that the boycott of schools and colleges should be carried on as effectively as before. I defer from the Civil Disobedience Enquiry Committee when they propose the abandonment of the withdrawal of boys from such schools and colleges. The question to my mind is of vital importance. It is on the youth of the country that the cause of *Swaraj* largely depends—and what chance is there for a nation which willingly, knowingly sends its boys, its young men to schools and colleges to be stamped with the stamps of slavery and foreign culture? I do not desire to enter into the question more minutely. I have expressed my views on the subject so often that I find it unnecessary to repeat them. I, however, agree with the recommendation of the Enquiry Committee that national schools and colleges should also be started.

"With regard to the question of the boycott of lawyers and the legal institutions I agree with the main recommendations of the Committee. Many questions have been raised as to whether the right of defence should be allowed or not and on what occasions, and for what purposes. I have never been in love with formal rules, and I think it impossible to frame rules which will cover all the circumstances which may arise in particular cases. All that I desire to insist on is the keeping in view of the principle of the boycott of courts."

Chittaranjan also talks about the importance of Hindu-Muslim unity in these words,

"With regard to the question of Hindu-Muslim Unity, untouchability and such matters, I agree with the recommendations of the Enquiry Committee. I desire to point out however the true unity of all sections of the Indian nation can only be based on a proper co-operation and the recognition by each section of the rights of the others—that is why I proposed that there should be a compact between different sections, between the different communities of India. We will do little good to the section known as untouchables if we approach them in a spirit of superiority. We must engage them in the work before us, and we must work with them side by side and shoulder to shoulder."

Concluding his speech, Chittaranjan finally spoke about the importance, which the symbol of *Khaddar* holds for the people of India. In his words,

"I now come to the question of *Khaddar* which I regard as one of the most important questions before us. As I have already said, I am opposed to the manufacture of *Khaddar* on a commercial basis. I said among the other things when I seconded the Bezwada resolution on the 31st of March in 1921 proposed by Mahatma Gandhi:

"'Our reason in asking the people to take to

Charka was not based upon any desire to enter into any competition with foreign capitalist production either from without or from within. Our idea is to enable the people to understand and fashion for themselves, their economic life and utilise the spare time of their families and opportunities with a view to create more economic goods for themselves and improve their own condition'. The idea is to make the people of this country self-reliant and self-contained. This work is difficult but essential and should be carried on with all our strength. I would much rather that few families were self-contained than that factories were started on a large scale. Such factories represent a short-sighted policy, and there is no doubt that though it would satisfy the present need it will create an evil which it would be difficult to eradicate. I am naturally opposed to the creation of a new Manchester in India of which we have had sufficient experience. Let us avoid that possibility, if we can.

"It is often stated that *Khaddar* alone will bring us *Swaraj*. I ask my countrymen in what way is it possible for *Khaddar* to lead us to *Swaraj*? It is in one sense only that the statement may be true. We must regard *Khaddar* as the symbol of *Swaraj*. As the *Khaddar* makes us self-contained with regard to a very large department of our national life, so it is hoped that the inspiration of *Khaddar* will make the whole of our national life self-contained and independent. That is the meaning of the symbol. To my mind such symbol worship requires the spreading out of all non-co-operation activities in every possible direction. It is only thus and only thus that the speedy attainment of *Swaraj* is possible.

"It remains to me to deliver to you a last message of hope and confidence. There is no royal road to freedom, and dark and difficult will be the path leading to it. But dauntless is your courage, and firm your resolution; and though there will be reverses, sometimes severe reverses, they will only have the effect of speeding your emancipation from the bondage of a Foreign Government. Do not make the mistake of confusing achievements with success. Achievement as in appearances are often deceptive. I contend that, though we cannot point to a great deal as solid achievement of the movement, the success of it is assured. That success is proclaimed by the bureaucracy in the repeated attempts which were made, and are still being made, to crush the growth of the movement, and to arrest its progress, in the refusal to repeal some of the most obnoxious of the repressive legislation, in the frequent use that has been made of the arbitrary or discretionary authority that is vested in the executive government and in sending to prison our beloved leader, who offered himself as a sacrifice to the wrath of the Bureaucracy. But though the ultimate success of the movement is assured, I warn you that the issue depends wholly on you and how you conduct yourselves in meeting the forces that are arrayed against you.... The forces that are arrayed against you are the forces not only of the Bureaucracy but of the modern Scribes and Pharisees whose interest it is to maintain the Bureaucracy in all its pristine glory. Be it yours to offer yourself as sacrifice in the interest of truth and justice, so that your children and your children's children may have the fruit of your sufferings. Be it yours to wage a spiritual warfare so that the victory, when it comes does not debase you, nor tempt you to retain the power of government in your own hands. But if yours is to be a spiritual warfare, your weapons must be those of the spiritual soldier. Anger is not for you, hatred is not for you, nor for you is pettiness, meanness or falsehood.

"For you is the hope of dawn and the confidence of the morning, and for you is the song that was sung by Titan, chained and imprisoned, but the champion of man in the Greek fable:

To Suffer woes with Hope, things infinite;
To forgive wrongs darker than death or night;
To defy power which seems Omnipotent:
To love, and bear, to hope till Hope creates
From its own wreck, the thing it contemplates;
Neither to change, nor falter, nor repent;
This like thy glory, Titan, is to be
Good, Great and joyous, beautiful and free;
This alone Life, Joy, Empire and Victory.
Bande Mataram" (Das).

❑

11

THE SWARAJ PARTY

The speech given at Gaya by Chittaranjan Das angered almost everyone who attended the session. After all, Chittaranjan had been talking about opposing Mahatma Gandhi and his idea of not entering the Council. Perhaps, Chittaranjan had a different view on this issue. He believed in resolving matters from the inside, rather than complete non-cooperation. He had wanted to enter the council and then change the government from within. This thought process had already begun to take shape when he was in prison for six months, prior to the Gaya Conference.

During his imprisonment, he met the great warrior of India, Subhas Chandra Bose. He started writing more poems and even wrote essays on Vaishnava philosophy and history of India's Nationalism, which were unfortunately not finished (Ray, 1927).

It was here in the prison when he first put across his idea of entering the Council and then showing their non-cooperation to the government. Below, is an essay written by Sk. Anwar Ali, which was published in a special issue of *Deshbandhur Katha* on August 15, 1982, to mark the thirty-fifth year of independence. In this essay, he gives an account of

Chittaranjan's prison experience.

"Deshbandhu's trial took place inside the Civil Jail for fear of great rush of people to watch the proceedings. He was given a six months' sentence and sent to the jail where he found his son, his friends and comrades, Subhas, Birendranath Sasmal Hemanta Sarkar, Maulana Abdul Kalam Azad and others. The annual session of the Congress was to be held at Ahmedabad and Deshbandhu was the President-elect. He sent his address through his sister and it was read in his absence by Sarojini Naidu. At the end of the session, Mahatmaji wanted to start a mass civil disobedience at Bardoli in Gujarat. But before he could launch the movement, an event of great violence occurred at a village called Chauri Chaura in U.P. where an infuriated mob retaliated on some policeman by setting the police station on fire and burning a number of policemen in it to death. This happened in February 1922 and Gandhiji promptly called off the movement in the whole country, to the pain, consternation, and amazement of almost all leaders, in prison or outside. Thus, ended the non-cooperation movement with Deshbandhu and many other leaders, including Pandit Motilal and Pandit Jawaharlal in prison. Very soon Mahatma himself was tried and given a long term of imprisonment.

"In prison Deshbandhu discussed his future programme and in these discussions council-entry figured prominently. His point was that council-entry was not inconsistent with non-cooperation. He believed—as he later demonstrated—that Reforms could be wrecked more easily and successfully from within than from outside. By entering the Councils, Congress could mend or end the dyarchical constitution. It was a question of strategy. Not everyone was convinced, and when he came out of the prison and started propagating and gathering the forces of public opinion round his scheme, he met with much hostility, both in Bengal and outside. But immediately on release, he did not start talking of the programme of Council-Entry on order to keep the word he had given to Pandit Motilal Nehru. In prison, his health had shattered and he went to Darjeeling to recoup his health. But Darjeeling did him no good and he decided to go to Kashmir, but he was not permitted to enter the State unless he gave assurance that he would not discuss political questions there. He refused to give this assurance" (*Deshbandhur Katha*, 1982, August 15).

Although many were against Chittaranjan's idea, he still found no reason to withdraw from his plan when he spoke at Gaya. Only a few agreed with him for the Council-Entry and when he founded his Swaraj Party, those were the only few who supported him.

Swaraj Party was formed by Chittaranjan, along with Motilal Nehru and Narasimha Chintaman Kelkar even before the Gaya Conference was over, much to the discontent of others. Chittaranjan did not look back. He was determined to reach his goal and thus, no one could change his mind. In 1923, Swaraj Party was the only thing on his mind and he did everything in his power to keep up the strength of the party.

On March 24, 1923, Lord Lytton wrote a letter which infuriated almost every Indian. In the following extract from the letter given below, Lord Lytton openly threatened Ashutosh Mookcrjce, who was the Vice Chancellor and Senate of the University of Calcutta. The issue was merely about the Amendment of the University Bill, in which Mr. Mookerjee had asked for changes.

"I should not complain of this if you declared

yourself an open antagonist and said to me frankly: 'In the interest of the University I am obliged to oppose your policy and cannot co-operate with you'. But in that case, you could not expect the government to retain you as a colleague and ask you to continue as Vice Chancellor.

"I invite you at this time when the Vice Chancellor's Office must be filled anew—a time which is also one of momentous consequences to the University—to assure me that you will exchange an attitude of opposition for one of whole-hearted assistance, for in our co-operation lies the only chance of securing public funds for the university without impairing its academic freedom.

"If you will do this, if you will work with us as a colleague and trust to your power of persuasion to get what you consider the defects in our Bill amended, if you can give an assurance that you will not work against the government or seek the aid of other agencies to defeat our Bill, then I am prepared to seek the concurrence of my Minister to your re-appointment as Vice Chancellor, and if you cannot conscientiously do this you must make yourself free to oppose me by ceasing to be Vice Chancellor."

This angered Mr. Mookerjee, and he replied Lord Lytton in an equal tone. An extract from his letter is given here:

"I claim that I have acted throughout in the best interests of the university notwithstanding formidable difficulties and obstacles and that I have uniformly tried to save your government from the pursuit of a radically wrong course—though my advice has not been heeded. I am not surprised that neither you nor your Minister can tolerate me. You assert that you want us to be men. You have one before you, who can speak and act fearlessly according to his convictions, and you are not able to stand the sight of him. It may not be impossible for you to secure the service of a subservient Vice Chancellor, prepared always to carry out the mandates of your government and to act as a spy on the Senate. He may enjoy the confidence of your government, but he will not certainly enjoy the confidence of the Senate and the public of Bengal. We shall watch with interest the performances of a Vice Chancellor of this type creating a new tradition for the office.

I send you without hesitation the only answer which an honourable man can send—an answer which you and your advisers expect and desire. I decline the insulting offer you have made to me."

Chittaranjan, at this time was helping Mr. Mookerjee with the issue of University Bill and therefore, these letters certainly must have aggravated him as well. He had been concentrating on how to put across the ideas of his Swaraj Party in front of the entire nation. Gaya Conference did not help him in this context, because most of them were against his plan of Council-Entry.

In a special Congress session held in Delhi in September, the same year, Mohammad Ali was presiding over it and he supported Chittaranjan's view and also said that Mahatma Gandhi agreed with Chittaranjan as well.

This gave him the satisfaction and confidence that he needed and he was soon able to gather enough members and funds for his party. The Swaraj Party met with success in the general elections held in Bengal and certain Central provinces and other areas.

Meanwhile, Chittaranjan also started a newspaper named *Forward* in order to reach out to a wider range of people.

When Lord Lytton asked Chittaranjan to form a

Ministry for the administration of the 'transferred' department, the latter could not wait to give him his reply. Chittaranjan sent Lord Lytton a letter on December 16, 1923, saying,

"I placed before our party the position as explained by your Excellency and they have just decided to accept your Excellency's kind offer. The members of this party are pledged to do everything in their power by using the legal right granted under the Reforms Act to put an end to the system of Dyarchy. This duty they cannot discharge if they take office. The party is aware that it is possible to offer obstruction from within by accepting office, but they do not consider it honest to accept office, which is under the existing system in your Excellency's gift, and then turn it into an instrument of obstruction. The awakened consciousness of the people of this country demands a change in the present system of government and until that is done or unless there is some change in the general situation, indicating a change of heart, the people of this country cannot offer willing co-operation. Under the circumstances, I regret I cannot undertake responsibility regarding the Transferred Departments. My party, however, wishes to 'place on record their appreciation of the spirit of constitutionalism' which actuated your Excellency in making the offer which they feel bound not to accept."

This was a sharp reply from Chittaranjan, and he was appreciated by everyone for it. He soon formed a coalition with the National Party. Everybody started showing their support to Chittaranjan again and this helped him with his mission.

❑

12

THE LAST TWO YEARS

In December 1923, Chittaranjan presided over the All-India Trade Union Congress which was held at Lahore.

Early next year, Chittaranjan made a whole new accomplishment. He wanted to have his own members in the Calcutta Municipal Corporation. The Corporation was to have a fresh constitution as a new Act was passed in 1923. So when the first election of this new setup was held in January 1924, Chittaranjan's party was the clear winner and he was elected as its first Mayor. This was a very big accomplishment for the Swaraj Party and they had the right to celebrate it.

On March 24, 1924, Bengal Legislative Council held a meeting in which the first motion for the demand of more than two-lakh rupees for the Minister's salaries was refused. This disappointed Chittaranjan so much that he later gave an answer to the Council when he put forth his opinion in the next Bengal Council meeting held in March 1925. According to him.

"It has been said that our cry is destroy, destroy. That our only point is destruction betrays such an utter ignorance of the Swarajist position that it is difficult to reply to it. Why do we want to destroy? What do we want to get rid of? We want to destroy and get rid of a system which does no good and can do no good. We want to destroy it, because we want to construct a system which can be worked with success and will enable us to do good to the masses. Can you lay your hands on your breast and say that you can do anything for the masses under this system? What have you yourselves done? It was tried for three long years with Sir Provash Chunder Mitter as one of the Ministers. May I ask in what way the condition of the masses has been improved? Has there been more education? Have they grown into anything? Has the province been better off financially? No. You have not got the power. And not having the power, you know that you can do no good in the present circumstances. It is a sham business altogether. On the one hand, the Ministers are Ministers endowed with responsibility and power and so on, but without funds they cannot do anything" (Ray, 1927).

Meanwhile, since the time Mahatma Gandhi had been imprisoned, non-violent activities had found its way in the minds of the young revolutionaries of Bengal. They became bolder and started using bombs and revolvers openly. In April 1924 at the Bengal Provincial Conference held at Serajgunge, the issue of the murder committed by Gopi Nath Shah of Mr. Daywas discussed. What is shocking is that, there were many sympathisers of Gopi Nath, who was not even remotely feeling guilty about his act. He justified it by saying that whatever happened may have happened even if he did not commit it. Since this issue was so heated, they even forced Chittaranjan to support the cause; although not for long. He was always against non-violence, and hence, he could not bear to accept this murder as a justifiable act.

During this time, at Tarakeswar near Hooghly, an issue regarding maladministration of the shrine arose and Chittaranjan had to look into its affairs. He formed a committee regarding this matter. Satyagraha was soon declared here and Chittaranjan then made a compromise with Satish Giri, who was the Mohunt of the shrine.

There is a short story narrated by Sailen Bishi, a follower of Chittaranjan Das, on this issue where he suggests how beautiful Chittaranjan's ideas were regarding this matter.

"I was with Deshbandhu when he was going to Tarakeswar from Howrah Railway Station. We were seated in the same compartment. Dr. Dasgupta was also accompanying us. When the train was on the move I thought to invite Deshbandhu's attention to communism. I told him, 'In Taskent the Communists have already occupied a strong position. This social system is sure to have its way to India very soon.'

"Deshbandhu said, 'I am not least worried if communism will find its way in India or not. I find a communist already seated before me.'

"I said, 'you may toy or speak idly, but this is sure to come.'

"In usual manner, I began to typify lectures on the exploitations of the capitalists, centralisation of capital, subjugation of the working classes, deception of the people in the name of religion, the uncivil attitude of the upper class—in short, all that I had gone through books, I cited without stop.

"Deshbandhu made a pause and then said, 'This European Communism cannot have any footing in India, as perhaps you do not actually know the heart of Indian Society. What you intend to import from foreign countries cannot grow here, even if it grows, it will be a good for nothing shrubbery.'

"Socialism is deeply rooted to the Indian way of life. India had no occasion to deprive other countries to get herself well-fed. She was seen to have distributed her wealth evenly to all. Earnings of well-to-do people were kept ready for the poor. Guests had no occasion to go without food. A kind of co-operative system was working in villages.

"The villagers as a rule made contributions for village ponds, temples, mosques, primary schools, tolls and maktabs to the benefit of all. The Zamindars of the villages were the trustees who were responsible to collect and disburse the funds. Disputes could be settled at the intervention of village panchayat. Folk songs, religious get-togethers, and various other entertainments were arranged towards improvement of culture and education of villagers. If the age long order was changed and newspapers or periodicals were given to work instead, if the system of joint family was abolished, and individual small families with selfish interest were allowed to grow, lots of complications might arise with changing social fashions which India could not afford or adjust. So it was a question of life and death to India which we must try to avoid. The visionary idea of the concept of *Swaraj* was that none would be in starvation, no one would be denied to have the full right to establish himself in the society. People would be at liberty to depend on each other for mutual benefit to create a society of real brotherhood. And you say centralisation of capital is the main root of all troubles and disputes. Of course this has been the order of present-day life. But in ancient societies, capital was never centralised. The system of distribution of wealth was not complex. As soon as the father of a family died, the entire wealth left by him was equally distributed among his sons. This repeated division of wealth was sufficient to maintain necessary adjustment of wealth in the society. The wealth and power of the merchant was thus restricted. Class struggle had no meaning for Indian society. Honest and simple was life.

"By the time we covered a long distance. At every station where there was a stoppage for the train, the school students with garlands and bouquets of flowers rushed into his compartment and greeted him. The Tarakeswar Railway Station was overcrowded soon. Swami Sachidananda entered the compartment. So our discussion had to be stopped.

"We found a sense of deep respect among the crowd. They came to welcome the leader who had launched a determined movement to restore the moral environment of the Tarakeswar temple by defeating the wicked design and harmful practice of the Mohant. We moved towards the temple. It took the heavy crowd half of an hour, ordinarily a distance of only five minutes' walk, to reach the temple. Due to density of multitude we could hardly move through. People in unbroken succession tried to touch his feet in respect. He attended the meeting of the action committee, then, went round for inspecting the arrangements and advised the leaders and workers on the future course of action. We came back to Calcutta by the evening train.

"During the Tarakeswar movement, his only son, Chiraranjan (Bhombal) was arrested and put into jail. Whoever was making any enquiry about his son in jail, Chittaranjan's reply was 'Bhombal is quite well.' He appeared to have no signs of anxiety in his appearance. Deshbandhu Chittaranjan Das was rather glad that his son was arrested and imprisoned.

"Sometime in the month of August, I went to meet Deshbandhu at his residence along with Sarat Chandra Chatterjee. Deshbandhu and Sarat Chandra were close friends. Sarat Chandra stepped inside Deshbandhu's room. I was waiting outside. After a while Chittaranjan had come out and seen me. He said, 'Why are you sitting outside? When did you come? Come in, come in.' He told Sarat Chandra, how was it that he had asked me to wait outside?

"....The revolutionaries of Bengal formed the subject of our discussion. He referred to some of the Detenus under Regulation III and gave his opinion about them. Finally, he concluded that violence was not the right answer. I asked him, 'Do you think that non-violence was not the right answer?' I asked did he actually believe that the country was in a position to win freedom through non-violence.

"Deshbandhu Chittaranjan said, 'When I was younger, I did not know about non-violence. But now I firmly believe that non-violence is the only way left to us.'

"He mentioned the names of a few detenus under Regulation III and said, 'They are really great workers, selfless patriots. They are prepared to give up everything for the cause of the country. We can work far better if they can join us. We can march ahead with our strength doubled.'

"At that moment the telephone was ringing. I came out and picked up the receiver. A very serious news—'Police firing at Tarakeswar'—Nayak office speaking—was the voice heard. I repeated the news in a louder voice to be heard by Chittaranjan and Sarat Chandra. Deshbandhu Chittaranjan and Sarat Chandra came out of the room. Deshbandhu Chittaranjan said, 'Don't get excited. Ask for the details. I am unable to follow the telephone message.'

I rang up 'Nayak' office again, they could not give me any further details and repeated the original message....

"After a while Lal Mohan Ghosh with two other Congress workers came to him to inform him of the shooting at Tarakeswar on the Satyagrahis by police. Deshbandhu Chittaranjan Das became sad to hear the news from them in details. He said, 'Innocent boys are shot at. The place of religion, a holy temple is involved in blood-shed. What else they intend to do?'

"It was already midnight. We all asked him to go to bed as he needed rest.

"He said, 'What you are talking of rest? I have on me the full responsibility of conducting such a massive movement. If we are defeated, it will be a state of disgrace for the whole of Bengal. Then again, the news of shooting. How to make time to take rest.'

"He discussed the situation up to 1 p.m. and advised us of the next programme. We bade him good night. When Sarat Chandra was coming out of his house, Deshbandhu Chittaranjan followed him up to the stairs. He attracted Sarat Chandra's attention to the idol of Shri Krishna made of black stone and began to narrate how he collected it. He told he collected the 500 years old image from Orissa. He intended to construct a temple to establish the image there. Then he said that he had a pair of Radha and Krishna with him which he wanted to make a present to Sarat Chandra. So saying, he went up again and came back with the set. He made it over to Sarat Chandra. It was a united image. He said, 'It is Janmastami (the birthday of Lord Krishna) today, then again there has been shooting at Tarakeswar. Today, the Lord himself is going to your house, as if He is leaving Nanda's house and going to Gokul.'

"With a smile he recited:
'He who will kill you,
Is gaining strength in Gokul." (Sen, 1989)

In December 1924, a session of Congress was held at Belgaum, which was presided over by Mahatma Gandhi. Chittaranjan also attended that session. Then, in March 1925, he spoke at the Bengal Legislative Council meeting on the issue of Minister's salaries which was again raised this year. An extract from his speech has already been mentioned above.

During the end of March, he issued two manifestos where he explained his party's policies to everyone, as the British and some group of Indians had a misconception of them being supportive of revolutionary and violent activities. The first manifesto of Chittaranjan affected Lord Birkenhead, who was the Secretary of State at that time, and he thought this to be a perfect opportunity to take a fresh step toward co-operation. Chittaranjan, then referring to Lord Birkenhead's invitation, issued another manifesto from Bankipore, near Patna, where he had been resting because of ill-health. He said,

"Lord Birkenhead has invited me to go forward and to co-operate with the government in repressing the violence which I deprecate. I entirely agree with him that never will freedom be reached by violence, and, if I may say so, I devoted a considerable portion of my speech at the Gaya Congress to demonstrating that freedom has never come through acts of violence, and, as I value freedom, I am not only willing but anxious to devote a few years of life that yet remain to me in carrying on an active propaganda against an evil which is a standing menace to the establishment of *Swaraj*. But I would be wanting in my duty as a conscientious citizen if I did not point out clearly and unequivocally that all my efforts in this direction are bound to be ineffective unless a favourable atmosphere is created by the government.

"Lord Birkenhead begins by saying that the repression which the Bengal Act contemplated is the repression of crime, and he concludes that nobody who is not a criminal is entitled to express grievance against that legislation. When I speak of repression, I mean it in the sense in which that term is used by constitutional lawyers—the exercise by persons in authority of wide arbitrary or discretionary powers of constraint. English writers of constitutional law have expressed the view that, whenever there is discretion, there is room for arbitrariness; and discretionary authority on the part of the government must mean insecurity for legal freedom on the part of its subjects.... My grievance against the Bengal legislation is that it has empowered the persons in authority to usurp the functions of the court of law and to exercise wide arbitrary and discretionary powers of constraint.

"This, to my mind, is conclusive of the situation before us. I therefore venture in return to invite Lord Birkenhead to cause a searching enquiry to be made into the causes which have brought about the revolutionary movement in India and then to set about applying the proper remedy, so that there may be a radical and permanent cure of the disease. It is no use treating merely the outward symptoms. I appeal to the government to treat the disease itself and to apply the proper remedy.

"The government should recognize that, however mistaken the revolutionaries may be, however wrong and futile their methods and however criminal and reprehensible their acts, the guiding principle of their lives is sacrifice for the attainment of political and economic freedom for their country. The moment they feel, that at any rate the foundation of our freedom is laid by the government, I venture to assert that the revolutionary movement will be a thing of the past. I suggest in all humility that there should be a distinct and authoritative declaration by the government at the earliest opportunity."

On May 2, 1925, Chittaranjan delivered his final public speech. His health had been deteriorating ever since he came back from his six-month imprisonment, but this year his illness had reached its final stage. At Faridpore, in the Bengal Provincial Conference held on May 2, he gave this Presidential speech in Bengali. It was also translated into English. The speech is given below,

"Again and again has India asked: 'Which way lies Salvation?' In the dim past it was the obstinate questioning of the individual Soul weary of shadows and seeking for Reality. In the living present it is the tortured cry of the Soul of India—'Which way lies Salvation.'

"Let me put this question to you again so that we may obtain a clear vision as to what it is that we must accomplish.

"As with the individual so with the nation, the question is to find out the meaning of deliverance from bondage and, let me add, sin. It is a sin of those who forge the fetters of bondage; it is also a sin of those who allow the fetters to be forged.

"Many ideas have been presented—Self-Government, Home Rule, Independence and *Swaraj*—but these are all names unless the full implications are vividly realised, and in the process of such realisation must come a consideration of the method of attaining the object in view.

"There are those who declare in favour of peaceful

and legitimate methods. There are others who claim that without the use of force or violence *Swaraj* is impossible of attainment.

"I desire to offer only a few suggestions to help you in deciding these momentous questions. Let the Bengal Provincial Conference declare in no uncertain voice what is the national ideal of freedom, and what is the method it calls upon the country to adopt for the fulfilment of that very ideal.

"Independence, to my mind, is a narrower ideal than that of *Swaraj*. It implies, it is true, the negative of dependence; but by itself it gives us no positive ideal. I do not for a moment suggest that independence is not consistent with *Swaraj*. But what is necessary is not mere independence but the establishment of *Swaraj*. India maybe independent tomorrow in the sense that the British people may leave us to our destiny but that will not necessarily give us what I understand by *Swaraj*. As I pointed out in my Presidential Address at Gaya India presents an interesting but a complicated problem of consolidating the many apparently conflicting elements which go to make up the Indian people. This work of consolidation is a long process, may even be a weary process; but without this no *Swaraj* is possible. Herein lies the great wisdom of Mahatma Gandhi's constructive programme. It is unnecessary for me here to discuss that programme as we are all privileged to-day to hear his message from his own lips. With that programme, I entirely agree and I cannot but too strongly urge upon my countrymen to give it not merely an intellectual assent but practical support by working it out to the fullest extent.

"Independence, in the second place, does not give you that idea of order which is the essence of *Swaraj*.

The work of consolidation which I have mentioned means the establishment of that order. But let it be clearly understood that what is sought to be established must be consistent with the genius, the temperament and the traditions of the Indian people. To my mind, *Swaraj* implies, firstly, that we must have the freedom of working out the consolidation of diverse elements of the Indian people; secondly, we must proceed with this work on national lines, not going back two thousand years ago, but going forward in the light and in the spirit of our national genius and temperament. For instance, when I speak of order, I mean a thing which is totally different from the idea of discipline which obtains in Europe. In Europe the foundation of society and the government is discipline; and the spirit of discipline upon which everything rests is entirely military; and the discipline which has made England what she is today is also the same military type. It is not for me to decry European civilization. That is their way and they must fulfil themselves. But our way is not their way and we must also fulfil ourselves. Thirdly, in the work before us, we must not be obstructed by any foreign power.

"What then we have to fix upon in the matter of ideal is what I call *Swaraj* and not mere Independence which maybe the negation of *Swaraj*. When we are asked as to what is our national idea of freedom, the only answer which is possible to give is *Swaraj*. I do not like either Home Rule or Self-Government. Possibly they come within, what I have described as *Swaraj*. But my culture somehow or other is antagonistic to the word 'rule'—be it Home Rule or Foreign Rule. My objection to the word Self-Government is exactly the same. If it defined as government by self or for self, my objection maybe met, but in that case *Swaraj* includes all those elements.

"Then comes the question as to whether this ideal is to be realised within the Empire or outside it? The answer which the Congress has always given is 'within the Empire if the Empire will recognise our rights' and 'outside the Empire if it does not.' We must have opportunity to live our life,—opportunity for self-realization, self-development and self-fulfilment. The question is of living our life. If the Empire furnishes sufficient scope for the growth and development of our national life, the Empire's idea is to be preferred. If on the contrary, the Empire like the Car of Jagannath crushes our life in the sweep of its imperialistic march there will be justification for the idea of the establishment of *Swaraj* outside the Empire.

"Indeed, the Empire gives us a vivid sense of many advantages. Dominion Status to-day is in no sense servitude. It is essentially an alliance by consent of those who form part of the Empire for material advantages in the real spirit of co-operation. Free alliance necessarily carries with it the right of separation. Before the War a separatist tendency was growing up in several parts of the Empire, but, after the War, it is generally believed that it is only as a great confederation that the Empire or its component parts can live. It is realised that under Modern conditions no nation can live in isolation and the Dominion Status while it affords complete protection to each constituent composing the great Commonwealth of Nations called the British Empire, secures to each the right to realise itself, develop itself and fulfil itself and therefore it expresses and implies all the elements of *Swaraj* which I have mentioned.

"To me the idea is specially attractive because of

its deep spiritual significance. I believe in world peace, in the ultimate federation of the world; and I think that the great Commonwealth of Nations called the British Empire—a federation of diverse races, each with its distinct life, distinct civilization, its distinct mental outlook—if properly led with statesmen at the helm—is bound to make lasting contribution to the great problem that awaits the statesman, the problem of knitting the world into the greatest federation the mind can conceive, the federation of the human race. But if properly *led* with statesmen at the helm;—for the development of the idea involves apparent sacrifice on the part of the constituent nations, and it certainly involves the giving up for good the Empire idea with its ugly attribute of domination. I think it is for the good of India, for the good of the Commonwealth, for the good of the world that India should strive for freedom within the Commonwealth and so serve the cause of humanity.

"I now come to the question of method. In my judgment the method is always a part of the ideal. So that when we are considering the question of method we cannot forget the larger aspect of the object we have in view.

"Viewed in this light the method of violence is hardly in keeping with our life and culture. I am not suggesting for a moment that the History of India shows no wars, nor the application of violence. Every superficial student of our history knows that it is not so. But sometimes things are forced upon our life which a critical student of our history must know how to separate from the real bent of our genius. Violence is not a part of our being as it is of Europe. That violence in Europe is checked by a system of law which in the ultimate resort is also based on physical force. The Indian people have always been in the habit of following traditions and customs and thus keeping itself free from violent methods. Our village organisations were a marvel of non-violent activities. Our institutions have always grown naturally like the unfolding of a flower. Strifes there have been of the intellect. Cravings there have been of the Soul. Disputes and quarrels have always arisen but only to be settled by peaceful arbitration. Anything contrary or antagonistic to this temperament is a method which is not only immoral from the highest stand point but is bound to fail. I have no hesitation in proclaiming my conviction that our freedom will never be won by revolutionary violence. In the next place, apart from the special psychology of the Indian mind, how is it possible, by offering such violence, as it is possible for a subject race to offer, to contend against the highly organized governmental violence of the present day? It is no use quoting the incidents of the French and other Revolutions. Those were days when people fought with spikes and often won. Is it conceivable that at the present moment we can overthrow any organized government of the modern type by such method? I venture to think that any such armed revolution would be impossible even in England to-day.

"In the next place, the application of violence cuts at the root of that consolidation without which as I have said the attainment of *Swaraj* is impossible. Violence is sure to be followed by more violence on the part of the government and repression maybe so violent that its only effect on the Indian people would be to check their enthusiasm for *Swaraj*. I ask those young men who are addicted to revolutionary methods,—do they think that the people will side with them? When life and property is threatened, the inevitable result is that the people who suffer or who think they may suffer recoil from such activities. This method therefore is impractical. Far be it for me to say one word against the honesty of purpose or the order of patriotism which these young men are capable of showing. But as I have said the method is unsuited to our temperament, therefore the application of it is to quote the words of Mahatma Gandhi 'waste of time and energy'. I appeal to the young men of Bengal who may even in their heart of hearts think in favour of violent methods to desist from such thought and I appeal to the Bengal Provincial Conference to declare clearly and unequivocally that in its opinion freedom cannot be achieved by such methods.

"But if I am against the application of such methods, I feel bound to point out that it is the violence of the government which has to a great extent helped the revolutionary movement in Bengal. I believe it is Professor Dicey who points out that for the last thirty years there has been a singular decline among modern Englishmen in their respect or reverence for law and order and he shows that this result is directly traceable to modern legislation which has had the effect of diminishing the authority of the law courts and thereby imperilling the rule of law. In other words, violence always begets violence; and if the government embarks on a career of lawlessness for the purpose of stifling legitimate activities it cannot but bring into existence what Dicey calls 'a zeal of lawlessness' in the subject. The history of India and particularly of Bengal supports the observation of Professor Dicey.

"The Revolutionary atmosphere in India has not been created all on a sudden. In this country, as elsewhere, it has passed through several stages. The first period was one of unrest brought about by the cumulative effect of a *century* of administration solely maintained in the interest of England and the English people. The period of unrest was further continued and strengthened when India came under the Crown in 1858. From 1858 to the end of the century covering the better part of the Victorian Era, an alien Bureaucracy administered the affairs of this country in complete forgetfulness of the best interest of the Indian people. This period was principally noted for the carefully studied neglect of the real Indian interest and for the flouting of the opinion of an articulate and educated people. I do not for a moment deny that the administration in the country in the latter part of the Victorian era was sometimes punctuated by axe of benevolent despotism such as Lord Ripon's Repeal of the Vernacular Press Act, the inauguration of the Local Self-Government, the Ilbert Bill and the Revision of the Indian Council Act, 1891 during Lord Lansdowne's viceroyalty. I call these acts of benevolent despotism because the underlying feature of most of them was the consolidation of the power of the Bureaucracy. The only measure of real importance was the Local Self-Government but if one carefully studies it one finds that it is not what it pretends to be. Real power was never parted with even when measures were adopted which superficially considered maybe supposed to be for the good of the people. On the other side, measures like Lord Lytton's Vernacular Press Act, the contemptuous reference to Lord Dufferin to the growing intelligentsia of India as 'a microscopic minority' and the niggardly grant for famine relief—now and again—prepared the soil upon which the revolutionary mentality of her later day was built up.

"Lord Curzon, however, inaugurated the second

stage or the stage of revolutionary mentality by the blazing indiscretions of his inglorious viceroyalty. He was the one, who for the first time set up the fetish of administrative 'efficiency' and placed it above the requirements of the people. On the other hand, he set up this fetish; on the other he began to flout Indian public opinion in the most persistent and obnoxious way. Circular after circular were issued to counteract and stifle national movements leading to the inauguration of the policy of repression and tyranny—repression and tyranny on one side and the foundation of a real revolutionary mentality among a section of the Indian intelligentsia on the other.

"After Lord Curzon the third stage was reached when the revolutionary mentality induced some youth to translate their feverish anxiety for retaliation and freedom into real revolutionary activities. During Lord Minto's viceroyalty the government showed its mailed fist and, with the velvet gloves taken off, a reign of terror was started. A section of the Bengal young men attempted to reply to this reign of terror by the free use of bombs and revolvers.

"One notable feature of this new psychology ought not to be forgotten or lost sight of if the question has to be studied from a broader point of view. The foundation of Indian unrest and of a revolutionary mentality has no doubt been laid by the persistence flouting of the Indian people and by a policy of repression and tyranny. But one is bound to admit that the success of the Japanese over the Russians in the bloody war about the end of the last century and the consequent reawakening of Asia, the Guerrilla Campaign of the Egyptian Nationalistics and the activities of the Irish Republicans and the subsequent foundation of the Soviet Russia with its world-wide Bolshevik propaganda and lastly the success of the Angora Government in bringing the English and the Greeks down to their knees,—has contributed not a little to the conviction that India's freedom must be won by whatever means possible."

Chittaranjan then read out the leading events in India from 1905 to 1909 and also talked briefly about the recent events. After this, he continued,

"It is thus clear that repression was followed by revolutionary movement which again was followed by further repression and that even when the British Government allowed measures which may be described as benevolent, they were always attended by others of a repressive character.

"With the Jallianwallah Bagh tragedy was started the new era in which Mahatma Gandhi initiated a propaganda of non-violent activity as a new way to fight for India's freedom. Let us hope that the whole of India has accepted it and I would press both upon the government and my revolutionary friends the utter futility of violence in any shape or form.

"The new Ordinance Act is a misguided attempt to perpetrate violence upon the people. The whole of India has with one voice condemned it and I cannot trust myself to express my feeling about it in fitting terms as I desire to speak with all restraint. I shall content myself by saying that I unhesitatingly condemn it and I have given the only answer which it is possible for any Indian to give to the recent speech of Lord Birkenhead inviting mc to co-operate with the government in its repressive policy.

"You will remember that Lord Birkenhead said that the Ordinance has not hurt anybody but the criminals. May I point out that His Lordship here is begging the whole question? We deny that the men imprisoned under the Ordinance are criminals and the only way to decide as to whether they are criminals or not is to hold an open trial and proceed not on secret information but on actual evidence which might be tested in open Court. The insecurity to which eminent writers of Constitutional history in England have referred is the insecurity to the public by attempt of the Executive to arrogate itself the position of a Court of Law.

"I will not weary you by dealing with each particular case which has been brought forward by the government as a justification for the policy of repression. Pandit Motilal Nehru in his speech in the Legislative Assembly on the Bengal Ordinance on February 25 last has dealt with it exhaustively and I ask every one of you to read that speech if you have any doubt on the point that there has been put forward no instance upon which the government can possibly substantiate this unjust claim. I must also point out that it is difficult to believe in the statement put forward in support of the repressive measures by the government. I shall quote only one instance and I have done. Speaking of the arrest and detention of the nine Bengali gentlemen including Srijut Krishna Kumar Mitter and late Ashwini Kumar Dutt on December 11, 1908, Lord Morley, the then Secretary of State, in his letter to Lord Minto stated as follows:

"'You have nine men locked up a year ago by *lettre de cachet*, because you believed them to be criminally connected with criminal plots, and because you expected their arrests to check these plots.'

"But let us hear what Hugh Stephenson has to say on the point. It is only the other day that he said from his place in the Bengal Council:

"'I should like to mention three cases which have

been used in the press to throw doubt on the efficiency, if not on the *bona fides* of our methods. The first two are those of Babu Ashwini Kumar Dutt and Babu Krishna Kumar Mitra. It has been said that no one will believe that they had anything to do with terrorist crime and therefore the secret information of the police must have been false and the government may equally well be deceived by such false information now. I never knew Babu Ashwini Kumar Dutt, but I am glad to think that Babu Krishna Kumar Mitra is a personal friend *and I entirely acquit him of sympathy with terrorist crime.* But as far as I know *none has ever accused him or Babu Ashwini Kumar Dutt of promoting crime, still less of taking part in it. The Bengal Government asked for the use of regulation III in the case of Babu Ashwini Kumar Dutt because of his whirlwind campaign of anti-government speeches.*'

"It follows conclusively that the discretionary power which the government in this country enjoys of promulgating illegal laws escapable of being abused. Indeed, it must be so from the very nature of things. The history of the world shows that the bureaucratic governments have always tried to consolidate their power through the process of 'Law and Order' which is an excellent phrase, but which means, in countries where the rule of law does not prevail, the exercise by persons in authority of wide arbitrary or discretionary powers of constraint. Repression is a process in the consolidation of arbitrary powers—and I condemn the violence of the government—for repression is the most violent form of violence—just as strongly as I condemn violence as a method of winning political liberty. I must warn the government that the policy of repression is a short-sighted policy. It may strengthen its hands for the time being, but I am sure, Lord Birkenhead realises that, as an instrument of government, it is bound to fail.

"I have so far dealt with the question of method in order to show that violence is both immoral and inexpedient,—immoral, because it is not in keeping with our life and culture, inexpedient, because it is inconceivable that at the present day we can overthrow any organised government by bombs and revolvers. Then the question arises what method should we pursue in order to win *Swaraj*? We have been gravely told that *Swaraj* is within our grasp if only we co-operate with the government in working the present Reform Act. With regard to that argument, my position is perfectly clear, and I should like to restate it, so that there may be no controversy about it. If I were satisfied that the present Act has transferred any real responsibility to the people,—that there is opportunity for self-realisation, self-development and self-fulfilment under the Act—I would unhesitatingly co-operate with the government and begin the constructive work with the Council Chamber. But I am not willing to sacrifice the substance for the shadow. I will not detain you to-day with any arguments tending to show that the Reform Act has not transferred any responsibility to the people. I have dealt with the question exhaustively in my address at the Ahmedabad Congress, and if further arguments are necessary, they will be found in the evidence given before the Muddiman Committee by men whose moderation cannot be questioned by the government. The basis of the present Act is distrust of the Ministers; and there can be no talk of co-operation in an atmosphere of distrust. At the same time, I must make clear my position,—and I hope that the Bengal Provincial Conference—that, provided some real responsibility is transferred to the people, there is no reason why we should not co-operate with the government. But to make such co-operation real and effective two things are necessary; first, there should be a real change of hearts in our rulers, secondly, *Swaraj* in the fullest sense must be guaranteed to us at once, to come automatically in the near future.

"I have always maintained that we should make large sacrifices in order to have the opportunity to begin our constructive work at once; and I think you will realize that a few years are nothing in the history of a nation, provided the foundation of *Swaraj* is laid at once and there is a real change of heart both in the rulers and in the subject. You will tell me that 'change of hearts' is a fine phrase, and that some practical demonstration should be given of that change. I agree. But that demonstration must necessarily depend on the atmosphere created by any proposed settlement. An atmosphere of trust or distrust may be easily felt, and in any matter of peaceful settlement great deal more depends on the spirit behind the terms than the actual terms themselves. It is impossible to lay down the exact terms of any such settlement at the present moment; but if a change of heart takes place and negotiations are carried on by both sides in the spirit of peace, harmony and mutual trust, such terms are capable of precise definition.

"A few suggestions may, however, be made having regard to what is nearest to the hearts of the people of Bengal. In the first place, the government divest itself of its wide discretionary powers of constraint, and follow it up by proclaiming a general amnesty of all political prisoners. In the next place, the government should guarantee to us the fullest recognition of our right to the establishment of *Swaraj* within the commonwealth, in the near future, and that in the meantime, till *Swaraj* comes, a sure and sufficient foundation of such *Swaraj* should be laid at once. What a sufficient foundation is and must necessarily be a matter of negotiation and settlement—settlement not only between the government and the people as a whole but also between the different communities not excluding the European and Anglo-Indian communities, as I said in my Presidential Speech at Gaya.

"I must also add that we on our part should be in a position to give some sort of undertaking that we shall not by word, deed, or gesture encourage the revolutionary propaganda and that we shall make every effort to put an end to such a movement. This undertaking is not needed, for the Bengal Provincial Conference has never identified itself with the revolutionary propaganda. I believe that with the change of heart on the part of the government, there is bound to be produced a change in the mental outlook of the revolutionary, and with the settlement such as I have described, the revolutionary movement will be a thing of the past, and the very power and energy which is now directed against the government will be devoted to the real service of the people.

"If, however, our offer of a settlement should not meet with any response; we must go on with our national work on the lines which we have pursued for the last two years so that it may become impossible for the government to carry on the administration of the country except by the exercise of its exceptional powers. There are some who shrink from this step, who point out with perfect logic that we have no right to refuse supplies unless we are prepared to go to the country and advise the subject not to pay the taxes. My answer is that I want to create the atmosphere for national civil disobedience, which must be the last weapon in the hand of the people striving for freedom. I have no use for historical precedent; but if reference is to be made to English history in our present struggle, I may point out that refusal to pay taxes in England in the time of the Stuarts came many years after the determination of the parliament to refuse supplies. The atmosphere for civil disobedience is created by compelling the government to raise money by the exercise of the exceptional powers; and when the time comes we shall not hesitate to advise our countrymen not to pay taxes which are sought to be raised by the exercise of the exceptional powers vested in the government.

"I hope that time will never come—indeed I see signs of a real change of heart everywhere—but let us face the fact that it may be necessary for us to have recourse to civil disobedience if all hopes of reconciliation fail. But let us also face the fact that civil disobedience requires a high stage of organization, an infinite capacity for sacrifice, and a real desire to subordinate personal and communal interest to the common interest of the nation: and I can see little hope of India ever being ready for civil disobedience until she is prepared to work on Mahatma Gandhi's constructive programme to the fullest extent. The end, however, must be kept in view, for freedom must be won.

"But, as I have said, I see signs of reconciliation everywhere. The world is tired of conflicts, and I think I see a real desire for construction, for consolidation. I believe that India has a great part to play in the history of the world. She has a message to deliver and she is anxious to deliver it in the Council Chamber of that great Commonwealth of Nations of which I have spoken. Will British statesmen rise to the occasion? To them I say, you can have peace to-day on terms that are honourable both to you and to us. To the British community in India, I say, you have come with traditions of freedom, and you cannot refuse to co-operate with us in our national struggle, provided we recognize your right to be heard in the final settlement. To the people of Bengal I say, you have made great sacrifices for daring to win political freedom and on you has fallen the brunt of official wrath. The time is not yet for putting aside your political weapons. Fight hard, but fight clean; and when the time for settlement comes, as it is bound to come, enter the peace conference not in a spirit of arrogance, but with becoming humility, so that it may be said of you that you were greater in your achievement than in adversity. Nationalism is merely a process in self-realization, self-development and self-fulfilment. It is not an end in itself. The growth and development of nationalism is necessary so that humanity may realise itself, develop itself and fulfil itself; and I beseech you, when you discuss the terms of settlement, do not forget the larger claim of humanity in your pride of nationalism. For myself, I have a clear vision as to what I seek. I seek a federation of the states of India: each free to follow, as it must follow, the culture and the tradition, of its own people: each bound to each in the common service of all: a great federation within a greater federation, the federation of free nations, whose freedom is the measure of their service to man, and whose unity the hope of peace among the peoples of the earth."

Next day, Mahatma Gandhi gave his speech at the same conference, where he spoke a few words in praise of Chittaranjan:

"I read the address of Deshbandhu Das and I have had the privilege and pleasure of reading the English translation. I do not know which is the original, whether Bengali or the English translation, because Bengali scholars tell me that the Bengali version reads as sweet and as eloquent as the English version, but, in any case, I had the pleasure and privilege of having an advanced copy of the English address when I was in Calcutta with a brief, little, loving, sweet note from Deshbandhu that, if I could spare a few minutes, I should read that address. Well, I read from the start to the finish and I was wondering whether he had pilfered every sentiment from me. But I must confess to you that I saw that the language was not mine. The language was that of a scholar and not of a rustic who delights in calling himself a spinner, a scavenger, a weaver, a farmer and now even a *Namasudra*. And so I saw that the language was not mine, but the thoughts seemed to have been pilfered and so immediately I said to myself, if he would ask me to subscribe to it, I would have no hesitation in doing so without perhaps altering a single word or a single phrase....

"I want to look not at phraseology. I do not want to look at the language. I only want to look at the thoughts that under lie it and what he has said to us in that address. If we are true to ourselves, if we are true to the nation, if we are true to the policy that was enunciated for the first time in Calcutta in 1920 with all the great deliberation that we could bring to bear upon that policy, if we are to be true to that, then, there is absolutely nothing in that address to cavil at. And that address is a re-enunciation and an emphatic and unequivocal re-enunciation of the policy that was laid down for the first time in the history of the Congress in 1920."

❑

13

Religion and Superstition

Before moving on to the final days of Chittaranjan, one small chapter needs to be dedicated to what Chittaranjan thought about various religions, especially the Hindu religion.

Chittaranjan, as we now know was born into a Brahmo family. All his uncles and other family members followed the Brahmo rituals and rites. But did Chittaranjan believe in them too?

Chittaranjan was a Hindu and his bent toward Vaishnava philosophy, as is evident from his poetries, show how much of a non-Brahmo he was. As already mentioned, his poetries had somewhat angered the Brahmo members and they did not want to associate themselves with him. They did not even attend his wedding, although his ceremony was performed according to the Brahmo rites.

Also, Chittaranjan was fond of drinking and smoking. He had a good collection of foreign brandy and cigars before the Boycott period. The members of the Brahmo Samaj objected to these habits, and this was another reason for them to distance themselves from Chittaranjan.

Mrs. Mukerjea told the author about her grandfather's habits and more;

"His father was a Brahmo, but he reverted to Hinduism. When his mother died, he performed *shradh* in the Hindu way. He used to say, 'If I want to reform the Hindu Samaj or the caste system, widow remarriage...and so on, I need to do it from within. If I am a Brahmo, they will think I am not of the same religion, so I cannot interfere. So I want to be a Hindu and a reformer'. Sowhen my *pishima* (his daughter) got married, it was an inter-caste marriage but the ceremony was performed according to the Hindu rituals, without registration. In those days, it was legal to get married like that. This, even Mahatma Gandhi and Motilal Nehru followed later on; marriage to another caste and without registration. If one goes on doing something, it becomes customary....

"He used to have two drinks (alcohol) every day and in those days, alcohol was looked down upon.... One of his poems was about a prostitute and her sorrows. And this too was not accepted by the Brahmo Samaj people."

It is ironical because the Brahmo Samaj members were supposed to be forward in their thinking but they could not accept the modern thoughts of Chittaranjan Das. Mrs. Mukerjea pointed out that this was because there were many elderly members in the Samaj who were not so modern in their thoughts.

Chittaranjan Das wanted to break the inadequate rules of the Hindu society, by being a Hindu himself. It is the same policy that he applied when he wanted to change the government by entering the Council.

He wanted to alter the orthodox views of the people about their religion and this he thought of doing by remaining a Hindu. He believed that if he wished to change their mind-set, he had to do it from within. It was his view that if he belonged to another religion, the Hindus would not listen to his ideas regarding the old traditions and rituals which he thought were best not practiced.

This belief of Chittaranjan made him different from all the other reformers, who instead of changing what was already there, regarded starting something new as a better option.

If one cannot change the mind-set of the older generation and awaken them, then how can one imagine gaining success in any religious matter; such were the thoughts of our Deshbandhu. He was a true reformer, who wanted all generations to be on the same level regarding the religious practices; this he thought would ultimately help them get rid of the older and obsolete rituals and traditions.

Although on one side Chittaranjan was modern in his thinking regarding the old traditions of the Hindu religion, he carried one superstition along with him which he could not part with; and this was the practice of 'Planchette'. An author wrote about it in his book on Chittaranjan Das. Even Mrs. Mukerjea confirmed this practice of her grandfather.

This practice only shows that Chittaranjan believed in the traditional idea of re-birth and after-life. He performed this activity on a regular basis along with his friends merely to take decisions on important matters.

Who could have guessed that a man of such progressive views could have faith even in old beliefs? Perhaps, one can never understand such things.

❑

14

DEATH AND AFTER

"Today as we look on the year 1925, we cannot help feeling that if Providence had spared the Deshbandhu for a few years more, the history of India would probably have taken a different turn." Subhas Chandra Bose said these words for Chittaranjan, a few years after his death; the context of this statement is not known, yet, one cannot deny his immeasurable respect for Deshbandhu.

Chittaranjan had been unwell for a long time; as has already been said, since the time of his release from jail, he had become extremely weak. But by the beginning of 1925, his health deteriorated and his condition worsened. He started having fever at regular intervals which affected his physical strength to a great extent.

Mrs. Mukerjea recalls,

"My grandfather after coming back from jail became weak. He had some illness. He overworked himself and had stomach pain and fever every day. We do not know what it was. Diagnosis of cancer was not possible in those days. Maybe he had cancer. Nobody knows. He suffered after he came out of jail. Many people said he was poisoned in jail which was a rumour. He had those symptoms just because of overwork."

Chittaranjan was then advised by the doctors to go to Europe for better medical help, but he chose after a great deal of thought to go to Darjeeling for rest, when his friend, Mr. Nipendra Nath Sarkar invited him.

Mrs. Mukerjea also confirmed this,

"Mr. Sarkar, a friend asked him to come to Darjeeling and rest in his house. He thought maybe this change would make him feel better. He used to go to England by ship and rest there when he was practicing. That is where he wrote *Sagar Sangeet.* Whole year he used to work, and two months he rested; but that stopped when he left his practice and joined politics. The Congress Party later offered to send him to England via ship since he was accustomed to going by sea, and the party was willing to pay for it. But he did not take it. He went to Darjeeling, when his friend offered him his house."

In Darjeeling, he stayed with his wife in a house on Lebong Road which was called, 'Step Aside'. This was owned by Mr. Sarkar. Chittaranjan wanted to stay away from all political matters and other stress related work. He shifted thereon May 16, 1925, after the Fardipore Conference.

Once in Darjeeling, Chittaranjan certainly felt at peace. He used to take long walks everyday despite his weakness which was witnessed by the residents of the town. People have stated this to authors who have written Chittaranjan's biography.

Following is a note taken from a book written by Prithwis Chandra Ray on Chittaranjan Das,

"From the day he arrived there, he began to take very long walks up and down the hills. Though he was gradually picking up, the weekly fevers appeared with a persistent periodicity. He would not heed these attacks, but went about on foot for several miles every morning and evening" (Ray, 1927).

In the meantime Chittaranjan used to have regular visitors in the house. Early in June, Mahatma Gandhi visited him and they talked about the future of the Swaraj Party. Later Mrs. Besant also paid him a visit to discuss about some political matter. It seemed that whoever came to see him, politics was often the subject of their discussion. No doubt, even if he said that he wanted to stay away from work, it was hardly possible for him to follow his own words. After all, he was one of the greatest political leaders that the country had.

Chittaranjan had been showing improvement during the middle of June. Three to four days before his death, several visitors had commented that he looked better. But on the morning of June 15, Chittaranjan's temperature rose above normal and the whole day he complained of severe pain in his whole body. Next day in the morning, his pulse began to sink. This worried Basanti Devi and she became quite restless. During the afternoon, his heart started beating abnormally and he became unconscious and at 5.15 in the evening, he was declared dead by the doctor.

After hearing the news of Chittaranjan's death, the whole town came to the house to see him for the last time. He was to be taken back to Calcutta for the cremation ceremony but this could not happen before the next morning. From five in the evening until midnight, people in Darjeeling kept coming to pay their respect to Chittaranjan.

Next day at around seven in the morning, he

was carried in a casket to the railway station. It took them two hours just to reach the station. His casket was decorated with flowers which were brought by those who were walking in the funeral procession which had started from 'Step Aside'. The casket was then placed in one of the mail vans because there was no place in the normal passenger vans. At every station where the train stopped, there were thousands of people who had come to see him. This delayed the train in reaching its destination by a few hours. When the train reached Sealdah station in Calcutta, the scene was overwhelming.

Mahatma Gandhi stood at the beginning of a crowd of three lakh people who had come to attend the funeral procession. Even on the way to the cremation ground, people kept joining the procession and finally they reached the burning *ghat* at around four in the evening.

Mr. Garvin, a prominent British journalist described the funeral procession in these words:

"Amongst us only a few in a million can realize that the funeral of a popular leader in Calcutta last Thursday was the greatest and strangest scene witnessed anywhere in the British Empire for many a day. Covered with flowers, the body of Mr. Das was borne in procession through vast crowds to the burning *ghat* with the drumming and clanging and wailing of music and cries that are not as ours. Mahatma Gandhi, clad only in his loin-cloth, was carried shoulder-high to the place of fire and ashes. Grief for the dead leader mingled with enthusiasm for the living saint to spread a delirium of emotion. No hero-worship in the West compares with the vehement though often fugitive idolatry devoted in

India to any conspicuous man who can magnetize the religious or racial sentiment of the people. We must look on a mourning like this with sympathy and respect apart from any reasoned difference of ideas about the future of Indian Government."

On July 1, 1925, Chiraranjan, Chittaranjan's son, performed the *shradh* ceremony in their house where thousands of people had gathered. *Shradh* is a Hindu ritual which is carried out in honour of the deceased so that his soul rests in peace. People gather in the house and *pundits* perform the ritual and then food is served to the poor people.

When a noble man dies, many are affected. On such an occasion, it is natural for everyone to express their grief. Mahatma Gandhi said these beautiful words for Chittaranjan:

"Mr. Das was one of the jewels among the servants of the country. His service and sacrifice was matchless. May their memory ever remain with us and may his example inspire us to noble efforts."

Aurobindo Ghose also expressed his sorrow in these words,

"Chittaranjan's death is a supreme loss. Consummately endowed with political intelligence, constructive imagination, magnetism, a driving force combining a strong will and uncommon plasticity of mind for vision and fact of the hour, he was the one man after Tilak, who could have led India to *Swaraj*."

In an article, "Sacrifice of Deshbandhu was the Greatest Gift to the Cause of the Country" dated August 15, 1982, published in *Deshbandhur Katha's* special edition, K.P. Raghu Raj wrote,

"The basic principle which Deshbandhu practiced can be summarised from the quotation of Lord Krishna as follows:

Daridran Vara Kounteya
Ma Prajachhesware Dhanam.

This quotation is by Lord Krishna addressing the sons of Kunti. Translated into simple language, he says, 'Oh, the sons of Kunti, your duty is to look after those who are poor and who have nothing; please do not try to help those who have enough and who can fend for themselves.' While there may be a dispute about the era of Lord Krishna and Pandavas, there is no doubt however, that this was much earlier than the time of Marx, Lenin and Hegel. In one single statement and advice given to Pandavas, I am yet to see a better interpretation of modern communism. Deshbandhu's life and his activities what we have read and what we have been told, seems to me to be guided by this simple advice. He worked at the prevention of misery rather for multiplying places of refuge for the miserable. His happiness was his work because he never believed that happiness comes by seeking.

"Let me quote Mrs. Neli Sengupta: 'He was one of our greatest leaders. He sacrificed so much and died at such an early age. It is so terrible that the present generation forgets the sacrifices of its elders. Youth should remember what sacrifices Deshbandhu and the men of his time made. They will certainly hesitate to behave as they are doing now-a-days. It was not a light matter for Mr. C.R. Das, as he was then, to give up his wonderful practice, work which he must have thoroughly enjoyed and also the future of his wife and children. A married man does not sacrifice just his own life but those of the many who depend on him.

"Deshbandhu's unique personal sacrifices of luxury and comfort of his princely income and style of living, and indeed of all his earthly possessions, coupled with his large hearted humanism, had invested his image with an aesthetic glory. That also was an integral part of his total personality. High and low, rich and poor, even those who were his political opponents, were attracted by his sincerity of purpose and selfless devotion to the cause advocated by him. He had given his all and wanted nothing in return except freedom of his Motherland and the emancipation of his people from foreign yoke, and from hunger, ignorance, disease and squalor.'

"My intention here is not to compare this giant with other stalwarts because this would not be right. Hence, I would like to give an impression on the political aspect of his life and this is from no other person than Netaji Subhas Chandra Bose who was his close aide in the freedom struggle: 'Deshbandhu was not only an idealist and a visionary but also a statesman of highest calibre. Deshbandhu had in him the instinct, or the judgment, so necessary for political bargaining in full measure.'

"Essentially, he was the people's man. He secured the hearty co-operation in such a measure that it is very difficult to find a match."

Indeed, Chittaranjan was a man who sacrificed everything for his 'Motherland'. One can still understand his sacrifice of practice as lawyer, but when he donated all his property to open a school and a hospital for women, the whole country's respect for him doubled. According to some sources, this donation was made on November 6, 1924.

Today that property holds the Chittaranjan Seva Sadan, which serves both the poor and everyone else.

"He lived as an anchorite and died as such, and now he sits enthroned in the hearts of millions of people and will continue to claim his sovereignty for ages unborn." These were the words of Surendra Nath

Bannerjee, with whom Chittaranjan wasn't on the friendliest of terms during his lifetime.

Sarojini Naidu also had a few words to say for Chittaranjan, which are,

"Kingly was Deshbandhu Das in every impulse and gesture of his life, royal alike in the splendour of his bounty and the splendour of his renunciation. As the idol of the nation he served with unsurpassing devotion. To the generations of tomorrow, he will grow in to a radiant figure of historic legend and romance, a vital portion of epic beauty and grandeur of their spiritual heritage."

A few lines written by Rabindranath Tagore on Chittaranjan are quoted here,

"Thou hast brought with thee a deathless life, and that thou hast gifted on thy death."

Maulana Abul Kalam Azad had a rather different opinion about this great man. He believed that if Chittaranjan had lived a few more years, he could have saved the partition of India and Pakistan. He wrote,

"I am convinced that if he had not died a premature death he would have created a new atmosphere in the country. It is a matter for regret that after he died, some of his followers assailed his position and his declaration was repudiated. The result was that the Muslim of Bengal moved away from the Congress and the first seeds of partition were sown."

Chittaranjan Das was a personality, whom anybody could have misunderstood easily. It is interesting to know that even his wife had once refused to marry him thinking him to be a drunkard. But when her father talked about his qualities and asked her to trust him, she looked beyond the obvious and accepted Chittaranjan with all her heart.

If one could ignore his disciplined attitude and

those harsh words spoken against his enemies, one would understand why he said what he said. He was a romantic at heart with a dream of seeing India standing up on its own feet, where no one tells them what to do. It wasn't a Utopian dream, as India did stand up on its own, created a Constitution of its own, and even though it was a few decades after his death, his dream did come true and he watched it through the eyes of million others.

"Sleep, sleep through clouded moons, O sea, at last
Under a lonely sky; the eyelids close
Wearied of song. Held are the regions fast;
Mute in the hushed and luminous world repose.
I sit upon thy hither shore, O main,
My gaze is on thy face. Yet sleep, O sleep!
My heart is trembling with a soundless strain,
My soul is watching by thy slumber deep.
When shall I know thee who thou art, O friend?
When wilt thou wake? With what grand paean vast?
Lo, I will wait for thee. Thou at the end
Stretch out thy arms in some dim eve at last."
(*The Songs of the Sea*, XXIII)

❑

Bibliography

Deshbandhur Katha. (1982, August 15). Calcutta: Deshbandhu Chittaranjan Das Memorial Committee.

Das, C. (n.d.). *Freedom Through Disobedience.* Madras: Arka Publishing House.

Ghose, A. (n.d.). *Translations.* Sri Aurobindo Ashram Publication Department.

Ghosh, Y. (1972). *Bengal Provincial Conference 1917.* Calcutta: Firma K.L. Mukhopadhyay.

Grover, V. (1994). *Chittaranjan Das: Political Thinkers of Modern India.* Deep & Deep Publications.

Ray, P.C. (1927). *Life and Times of C.R. Das.* Oxford University Press.

Sen, R.N. (1989). *Life and Times of Deshbandhu Chittaranjan Das.* New Delhi: Northern Book Centre.